WAKING UP TO LOVE

To Kim & Desi,

With love,

Scarlett

Waking up to Love

Our Shared Near-Death Encounter Brought
Miracles, Recovery and Second Chances

Scarlett L. Heinbuch, PhD

Printed in the United States of America
First Printing, 2018

ISBN 978–1–947637–08–5 print edition
ISBN 978–1–947637–09–2 ebook edition

Near-Death Experiences, Shared Near-Death Experiences, Reiki, Spirituality, Christianity, Judaism, Paranormal, Natural Healing, Wegener's Granulomatosis, Granulomatosis with Polyangiitis

Contact Scarlett L. Heinbuch at: http://www.scarlettheinbuch.com

Waterside Press
2055 Oxford Ave
Cardiff, CA 92007
www.waterside.com

To our mothers:

David's mother: Dee Brodkin (Mama Dee) – March 27, 1942 – December 17, 2012
Scarlett's mother: Doris Russell

Thank you for giving us life and love and for being the light workers you are. Both of you are amazing healers.

Mama Dee helped thousands of people with recovery from alcoholism, addiction, and other issues and championed LGBTQ rights. She was an amazing woman whose wisdom, kindness, humor, and love shined through in everything she did.

My mother, Doris, was a career RN who devoted her life to healing, helping, and soothing the suffering. She learned Healing Touch and used it with her patients to help ease their pain. She prayed with them, and in many cases prayed for them, holding their hands when they died. She comforted their families. She continues to share her wisdom, love, kindness, and humor with us, and for that we are grateful.

Finally, we dedicate this to the God of our understanding, who is Love.

PREFACE

This book is about the unusual way I met my husband. It was a profound set of experiences involving near-death for him (he was in an unresponsive coma from a rare illness that cut off the blood supply to his major organs, including kidneys and lungs, and was on life support for about three and a half weeks)—and a transcendent experience for me through doing healing prayer and Reiki with him. It started when I met his mother and ended up visiting him. After I worked with him for 12 days, David recovered unexpectedly. During our first several days together, we had a shared near-death encounter that showed us a world of love that I can only imagine is what heaven feels like. This love has no words. It is all the kinds of love that a human can feel rolled into one; and that does not describe even only one particle of it. I hope to help you find the world of love we experienced in your life too.

Acknowledgments

David owes his life to the care he received during the fall of 2005 from the nurses and doctors of the Cardiac Care Unit at St. Mary's Hospital in Richmond, Virginia.

He also owes his life to the loving hands of his recovery friends in Alcoholics Anonymous. The people in the Richmond AA fellowship showed up, prayed, arranged travel for David's family, and provided meals, support, and care for David when he nearly lost his life. They shall remain anonymous in the spirit of the program's tradition, but you know who you are, and we love you and thank you.

A heartfelt thank you to David's professional colleagues, including Ralph Brugueras and Debra Rosenfeld, who showed us that great hearts exist in the corporate world. Kevin Custer-Shook and Carmen Vincent-Kesho, you two started out as colleagues who became and remain heartmates! I love you both.

For me, there are so many people to thank that I cannot possibly name them all here or it would be another book. But I would like to call out the following: Hugh Campbell, Gordon Sharp-Bolster, Gerry Daly, Susan Stubbs, Leah Ley, Kevin O'Connor, and Lynwood Jackson. Your friendships and support saved the day in every way.

Joanne Bibb, MSW, LCSW, my Usui Reiki Master/ Teacher, a million thanks for your love, guidance and healing throughout many years.

James Grieger, Chic K., Dr. Tracey Jackson, Dr. Hilda Meth, Dr. Lindley Smith, Douglas Scott Jones, Peggy Siegel, MS, Dr. Kay Johnson-Gentile: your love, healing hands, friendship, and support mean more to me than you'll ever know.

Linda Shelton, Faith Grieger, Sharon Machrone, Clare Myatt—ladies, you are my soul sisters who have walked with me through many steps of this life journey.

Rev. Nancy Detweiler, who provided the early editing and encouragement, your beautiful soul inspires so many, including me. Thank you for your faith in me and this book.

Greg S. Reid, thank you for all you do for so many, your relentless inspiration and for all you've done to help me achieve. You're amazing.

William Gladstone, thank you for paving the way for so many and having the courage to walk your truth, share it with others, and help others share theirs.

Kenneth Kales, thank you for your sensitive editing and expertise. Your warmth and caring spirit brought peace to me and provided the safe space to share my story.

Richard Crowder, Ph.D., thank you for your eagle eye and great support throughout the years.

Dougie Bowman-Scudder, thank you for loving the story and encouraging me to move forward with it all. You and Bob Scudder have been amazing champions and I am grateful!

Richmond legend, Shirley T. Burke, thank you for always keeping it real with me and for being my soul sister in every way.

Melissa Canaday, your friendship has been a major influence in my life. Thank you for your generous spirit and for sharing your Native American wisdom that benefits so many.

Other people for whom I am grateful for your influence and care: Chris Yousik, Dionne Henry, Elizabeth McClendon, Alesia Hollis, Patty Heinbuch, Ruth Stege, Wayde Heinbuch, and Susan M. Nelson.

This book was breathed into life with the amazing support of my Master Mind partners for the past seven years: James Kilgarriff and Ping Yang, Ph.D. Your ongoing faith and encouragement have enriched my life in countless ways. Thank you both.

Special thanks to the Napoleon Hill Foundation and Don Green, whose ongoing dedication to help others succeed is the key to moving forward in so many areas of my life.

To my students and guest speakers during the Marriage and Family classes of 2005 through 2006: we learned lasting life lessons together and I am forever grateful. David Vairo, student, colleague, friend—thank you for being you.

To those on the other side with heartfelt thanks and love: Cheryll Nachman, Thomas Heinbuch, M. Njeri Jackson, Ph.D., and George Ritchie, M.D.

To those in recovery all over the world, thank you for your courage to continue to live life on life's terms.

Finally, to our amazing children who went through this journey with us: we love you to the moon and back.

INTRODUCTION

People ask us all the time how David and I met. And when we tell them about David being on the brink of death in a multi-system organ failure and coma for nearly four weeks, about how I met his mother and went to see him, the Reiki energy I used, our shared near-death experience, the spoken healing prayers, and David's miraculous recovery, they say, "You should write a book!"

It's taken years to write it because we've been busy living with all the challenges that have come our way. Plus, one of the hardest things in telling any true story is to know how much truth to tell. I struggled with whether to reveal our recovery process in Alcoholics Anonymous and other 12-step programs. I didn't want this to be a book about AA or about outing the anonymity of others. I sought advice that ranged from "don't mention it" to "be honest because people are struggling." The truth is, were it not for AA, I would not have met David. While I met him first during our shared near-death experience and then again when he woke up, I was there because I'd met his mother at an AA meeting. I owe my life to the healing hands of AA, as does David. So, I am going to be honest about it.

In the end, however, there is another truth about what brought us together and what healed us both. Love brought us together. Divine love's guiding hand. The loving prayers of so many friends, family, and strangers in churches, AA meetings from coast to coast, and at David's bedside. The loving hands of the hospital staff at St. Mary's Hospital in Richmond, Virginia. The doctors, nurses, therapists, aides, housekeepers, chaplain, and all of the others who showed up to help.

There is a loving force field we merged into. We found this field unites us all if only we will listen to the whisper in our soul, nudging us to follow our heart even when we don't know where it will lead. This loving force is behind energy healings, such as Reiki and other energy approaches, and it allows us to connect spiritually with other human beings and to facilitate their healing process.

In the end, this is not a story about me being a great energy healer or David being a passive dying man on a bed who was somehow saved. No. This is a story about the healing power of love from one soul to another.

David's soul made the call and my soul answered. We both had choices. I could have ignored the call of my spirit. He could have chosen to leave this earth. And those choices would have been okay because we wouldn't have known what we missed. After all, we had never met. I would have gone on with my life. He would have gone on with his death and his spiritual journey.

But love stepped in—a mother's love. Mama Dee. And that's where this story begins.

I fell over a moon bridge
Searching for pennies and goldfish.

—David E. Schwartz, December 2005

Do not conform to the pattern of this world, but be transformed by the renewing of your mind. Then you will be able to test and approve what God's will is—his good, pleasing and perfect will.

—Romans 12:2 NIV

CHAPTER 1
THE MAN ON THE BED

People say time stands still when soul mates meet. It's the story of my life that I would finally meet my soul mate during what were supposed to be his dying days. I can't say we actually met, since he was in an unresponsive coma on life support knocking at death's door in the Cardiac Care Unit (CCU) at St. Mary's Hospital. I didn't even know he was the one at that time and wasn't sure what I could do, or why I was even there, but I had met his mother the night before and she had touched my heart.

My first impression of the bloated man on the gurney was that he didn't look human. Dark tufts of his hair poked through the tangled tubes and wires. The little I could see of his face was blocked by the breathing tube in his mouth, held in place by a large patch of tape pressing into his swollen lips. A clear feeding tube straddled his nose and a brown ooze lodged in the bend. His neck was connected to a swatch of needles hooked to the dripping IV lines while a catheter bag dangling by his side was so dry the sides stuck together in the middle. A thin white sheet was draped over him like a shroud in the chilly, dimly lit critical care room.

The only signs of life were the beeps of the heart monitor and the ventilator breathing for him in a whooshing rhythm, like a metronome set at a slow tick. For three and a half weeks he had settled into this condition. Now he was heading into his fourth week if he made it through the day. But no one thought he would.

I knew only that his name was David and that he knew several of my friends, including a man I really liked.

As for me, I was 45, divorced twice, and the mother of two children—each with major health issues. My oldest son, Ryan, had severe ADHD, and my youngest, James, had epilepsy. I struggled along as a single mom doing what I could to research and educate myself on how to help my kids function better, and hopefully to heal. It seemed the only thing I'd managed to do right at that time was to go to college so I could get better paying jobs and see if I could find answers for my boys. I had received a bachelor's degree at age 36, a master's in public health at 39, and decided to keep going. Now I was in a PhD program in public policy, all done but for the dissertation. Broke and stressed, I had struggled personally with everything from drinking to depression. My life was a train wreck and I had given up on love. But I had turned things around and was embracing living life on life's terms, accepting things as they came and enjoying the benefits of not drinking and recovery in AA.

It was ironic that I was teaching a college course on "Marriage and Family Relationships." The semester had just started and I was loving the class. I was certain I could learn some things for myself along with sharing what I knew about how complicated life, love, and relationships could be. I was also a graduate teaching assistant by day for two classes in criminal justice. Relationships gone wrong were often at the heart of crimes. The two were more connected than I had realized at the time.

I couldn't have known that the day I stepped into David's room would forever alter the course of my life. This dying man would teach me lessons about love, life, healing, and spirituality without ever speaking a word.

Though I could not anticipate that we would share in a near-death experience and wake up in another world of love on the other side that healed us both, I did know that life unfolds as a series of small choices, made second by second, that change our destinies. So there I was. I had gotten myself into this because I met this man's mother the night before at an AA meeting and her grief had touched me profoundly. I had altered my destiny when I blurted out words I still cannot believe I said to her.

Chapter 2
A Glimpse into My Past

I always believed that I was destined for something good regardless of what life doled out or how far from that path I strayed. My childhood was difficult. Relationships were a nightmare. I couldn't trust anything—not God, not myself, and certainly not all that I'd heard about soul mates. I was lost and clearly did not know who to trust or even how to discern who was right.

As a young child my quest for spiritual solace kept me searching out different churches and philosophies. On Sunday nights I went to church with my grandparents just so I could sing the Baptist hymns. I loved *Amazing Grace*. Wedged between my grandparents, sheltered in their love, I sang with gusto. I spent lots of time at my grandparents' house; it was one of the few places I felt safe and loved.

My earliest memories are a mishmash of confusion. I was born with an ability to intuitively know things without knowing how. Throughout the years I tried to understand how I could know things before they happened, or how I could see the truth of a situation without any prior knowledge, or how I could sense the presence of those who had passed on. I often didn't know how to interpret my childhood experiences as anything other than normal, although I could tell from the reaction of adults that I was anything but. Along with this intuition, I experienced a profound sense of love. I remember feeling embraced in this all-encompassing love that was so powerful my whole body would shake as if an electric current was racing through me. I was unable to contain it. My mother later wrote in her journal that "Scarlett loved so hard she could hardly stand it." I was about three or four then and the difficult years to come seemed to shut off my connection to that infusion of love.

My mom and dad had married in 1958. They were both really young; Dad was 19 and Mom was 22. Three children came in quick succession. My older sister was born; I arrived 13 months later, and my brother followed 18 months after me. Mom had finished nursing school in 1958 and worked at various nursing jobs. Dad worked at a local garage. He drank hard, hung out with his buddies, and chain-smoked cigarettes.

Dad's drinking often made him mean. He and Mom argued at times and I remember the fear and the queasy feeling in my stomach when they fought.

I also remember the relief I felt when my mom would pack us up to go to her parents' house. My grandparents would let us stay up late and watch The Carol Burnett Show, which I loved. Then we were tucked into bed. I could sleep but I had the sense that I was able to float around most of the night. I floated down the steps and around the house, through the back-porch door, down the steps, and over to Great Grandpa Kolbe's blacksmith shop built on the land behind my grandparents' house. Years earlier, Great Grandpa Kolbe shot himself in the head after learning he had advanced cancer. I had never known him in life. I didn't think much about these floating experiences during my childhood and didn't talk about them with anyone.

A few years ago at a family reunion, my cousin, who lived with my grandparents when we were kids, told the story that she and Grandpa were having a late lunch in the kitchen. I was supposed to be upstairs, napping, because I was about four or so and it was my naptime. Then all of a sudden, they both saw me standing in the kitchen staring at them. Grandpa asked me what I was doing out of bed and said I needed to get back there. He then clapped his hands. My cousin said I disappeared right in front of their eyes. They both jumped up from the table and ran upstairs, where they found me soundly sleeping. They were both shaken by this and it was not talked about until 35 years later when my cousin was telling stories about my childhood abilities. That was the first time I had heard this story.

We spent many nights and weekends with my grandparents. Some of my fondest memories are of filling bushel baskets with apples we had gathered from Grandma's orchard. Grandma was Pennsylvania Dutch. She made apple pies from the freshly gathered apples while supervising me as I learned to use the rolling pin to flatten the dough just right.

Grandpa said his mother was Cherokee from North Carolina. He thought I looked like her and always called me "his little powwow." Because I was pensive, he also called me "the wise old owl."

Grandma subscribed to *Fate* magazine and from time to time she would allow me to read it. I loved the spooky stories in *Fate*. They helped me to not feel so alone because the same things were happening to me. I could feel people who had died. The first three days after a family member died, I hated to be alone because they would usually pay me a visit and it scared me. I slept with my head under the covers, petrified. It was hard to breathe, but the fear was worse. Even under the covers, when the dead people as a whole didn't visit, their faces still came. I could see all sorts of faces: some scary, some nice, but most of them looked terrifying. And it didn't matter that I squeezed my eyes shut. I saw them anyway. They wouldn't leave me alone.

Other things had happened, too. I always seemed to know things that were going to happen or were already happening somewhere else. It had become the norm for me and I just thought everyone knew things like I did. One day, I was riding in the car with Mom, Dad, and my siblings. I usually rode in the middle of the back seat. Both Cheryl and Will would be tired and want to take a nap in my lap. Sometimes I was tired, too, but they needed someone to take care of them, so that's what I did. Our family was headed to a park or some other outing.

It was a hot summer afternoon; the windows were rolled up in the car with the air conditioning blowing. I was looking out the window at the trees and all of a sudden, the trees were replaced with me seeing my Uncle Howard, Dad's brother, standing at the front door of our house reaching up to knock on the door. I saw him knocking several times, looking annoyed that no one answered.

"We need to go home," I said to my parents. "Uncle Howard's at our house."

"Uncle Howard's not coming to our house today, honey," Mom said.

"Yes, he is Mama. He's there now," I insisted.

My parents reassured me that we had no plans to see Uncle Howard that day, so we drove on. A few hours later, we went home. There was a note sticking out from the door of our gray house. It was from Uncle Howard. "Just dropped by. It's around 2. Call if you want to come see us tonight." No one said anything.

That night I crawled into bed, then pulled the covers over my head, knowing the faces would come and the whispering would begin. I couldn't understand anything they said; they just flashed up in my mind. It scared me with my eyes closed, but I was afraid too that if I peeked out from under the covers I would see some of them standing by my bed.

I was scared of the dark and begged for a nightlight. Mom bought me one, but it didn't chase the darkness away and it didn't stop the visits. My stomach clenched in fear every night. Eventually I drifted off to sleep. Mom said they would often find me in the morning sleeping face down but in a crouch, with my legs drawn up to my belly and my butt sticking in the air as though I had been dropped down from the ceiling and landed that way.

Not long after I started kindergarten at the school near my grandparents, who would drive me there and pick me up each day. My cousins lived with my grandparents, so it was fun. I looked forward to laughing at Carol Burnett and attending the church where I could sing. Laughter and God got me through tough times.

The years wore on and I focused on working hard. I started babysitting at 12 and then got a job at a local hamburger stand when I was 14. I worked there throughout high school, eventually managing the shop and closing it in the evenings. I also worked at a local retail store when I wasn't working at the hamburger place. I had saved my hamburger money to buy my first car at age 16. I opened my own checking account and paid my own way.

I also volunteered at a local crisis center, working in the afterschool program for city kids. The crisis center had a hotline too for runaway kids. One of the center directors, Stan, a retired physicist, was very interested in the technique of remote viewing that Stanford University was actively researching. Remote viewing was used by NASA and the U.S. government and is a technique in which a person can be trained to sense remote locations and describe what they see there. I could talk to Stan about my abilities, and we experimented with remote viewing to see if I could sense where a runaway had gone. I was not very good at locating the runaway. However, something unexpected did happen. I felt a sense of love for the runaway and connected with him or her. I sent a message of love, that all was forgiven, and to call home. In about six of the ten cases we focused on, the teen called home within an hour. Maybe it was just chance.

I finished high school at 17, turned 18 in the summer and left home. I moved to Richmond, met a nice guy, and got married at 22. We lived in Old Town, Alexandria, and went out a lot and drank too much. The marriage lasted until I was 25. Then I moved to Virginia Beach to work at The Association for Research and Enlightenment (A.R.E.) that was based on the work of the famous psychic Edgar Cayce. I chose Virginia Beach because it was still in Virginia, I was fascinated by the work of Edgar Cayce, I had heard many psychics lived there, and I was trying to find a place where I could be accepted and where I could feel at home. I worked in the audio-visual department writing blurbs for some of the teaching CDs along with processing horoscope chart requests. At night, I worked as a cocktail waitress to supplement my income.

Later, I moved into bartending and the owner asked me to manage the night shift. It wasn't long before I left the A.R.E. and began living the whole bar scene. I met a local fellow and we struck up a relationship that was a mismatch from the beginning. When I later got pregnant, I chose not to marry him—it just didn't feel right.

I moved to Norfolk and was working at a local pub, but was fired from my job when I was seven months pregnant. I went to Social Services for help and couldn't believe that I was now a welfare mom. How had this happened? I was also enrolled in nursing school and thought I was getting my life together. I wasn't ready for a baby, yet I was also excited and happy and scared all at the same time. I had no idea what the years would bring or what challenges would lie ahead.

When Ryan was born in 1988 he suffered from birth complications. Upon delivery, he wasn't breathing and an emergency breathing tube had to be used to help clear his airway. The doctors warned me there might be problems due to the oxygen deprivation he had experienced when he went into fetal distress. Yes, there were problems right from the beginning. Consumed with Ryan's needs, I dropped out of nursing school. A few years later when he was two, he was also diagnosed with severe Attention Deficit Hyperactivity Disorder (ADHD). I had stayed with Ryan's father for a time but moved when Ryan was 18 months old.

By 1991 I had moved to Richmond. There I met a man at a church dinner. I thought God had sent him to me. At first he appeared to be a loving, kind man who wanted to be there for me and to help Ryan. Instead, he turned out to be a bigamist and a con artist—a fact I learned after about six weeks when three of his former wives appeared on the Sally Jessy Raphael show. I was horrified. He had stolen some checks from my checkbook and cleaned out what little money I had.

The local newspaper crime reporter, Tim, covered the story. He and I developed a friendship, at first largely because I had always wanted to be a journalist and he encouraged me to follow that dream. At the time, I was working as an executive secretary at a local university hospital and was going to school two nights a week to earn my college degree. As our friendship grew into something more, I thought maybe God had put this experience in my life to bring Tim and me together. We got married in 1993 and he adopted Ryan. We had a son together in 1995 whom we named James. This little boy was angelic. At last, I thought. The white picket fence, the house, and a family. Life would turn out good after all. But it was not meant to be.

We struggled for years with Ryan's educational and medical needs—so much so that our family life had been drained to the breaking point more times than I can recall. At age 5, Ryan was placed in special education in public school kindergarten. Those years were a blur of nonstop meetings. Every year an "Individualized Education Plan" (known as an IEP) was required. These plans did nothing more than authorize restraints, or visits to the "quiet room," which looked like a small cell where our son seemed to be spending progressively more time while falling further behind in his academics. In addition, he had attended special schools as a part of the repeated hospitalizations brought about by his behavioral explosions, which the doctors attributed to adverse reactions to medications.

Ryan was seven when James was born. I knew he was excited to have a baby brother, but his chemical imbalance made the adjustment difficult and his behavior toward our newborn became increasingly threatening.

All of these experiences took their toll. Tim and I were fighting from the strain. He blamed me for Ryan's behavior and our little family began to crumble. My husband increasingly lost patience with Ryan and was quick to yell at him or lose his temper, which just set Ryan off even more. I felt trapped in this nightmare, not sure what to do or how to protect my sons.

Ryan was eight at his next hospitalization. The doctors observed him for three days and called us in for a meeting to discuss his diagnosis. They told us there was no hope. Ryan was born with "crossed wires" in his brain, a victim of unfortunate genetics. There was no medication that could help and the more than twenty medications that had already been used had only made him worse. There was nothing more to be done.

They advised us to make him a "ward of the state," which would mean turning him over to the state and abdicating our parental rights. Better to cut the ties now and get on with life, they added. Besides, our younger son needed us, as did our marriage which was on the rocks from the relentless strain. As the doctors went on, I began sobbing uncontrollably, feeling my heart breaking at what felt like a death sentence for my son. When Tim and I walked to the parking lot, he said he had to get back to work.

Tim and I had driven separately to the meeting because he had left work to come. He left me in the parking lot, still crying so hard that I could barely see to drive home. I felt that Tim had abandoned me when I needed him most and now I was on my own. I was sick with fear for the future. I somehow made it home and literally stumbled in and fell to my knees. I prayed to God to help me find answers for my sons. In addition to coping with Ryan's needs, James was diagnosed early on with petit mal epilepsy and was having 20 seizures a day, in which he would freeze and stare, his eyes blinking rapidly. I was beside myself with anguish and wanted to help my children.

I refused to accept their assessment. I would not give up on Ryan, no matter what the doctors said.

I spent the next several years researching at the Tompkins-McCaw Library for the Health Sciences at

Virginia Commonwealth University. I researched foods, chemicals, diets, fatty acids, energy treatments, spiritual philosophies, and anything that I thought might help my boys. I began and completed a master's degree in public health in a little over one year, which helped me to fine-tune my research skills. My thesis was on the nutritional and physiological aspects of brain-based disorders.

Despite my appearance of outward progress, inside I was extremely depressed and seriously wondering why I was alive. I was even contemplating suicide. My marriage was ruined and I couldn't help my children. I felt I'd failed as a wife, mother, and person. I tried medication for my depression, but couldn't tolerate it. Soon after, a glass of wine with dinner turned into finishing the whole bottle. In addition to being depressed, I began to worry, *am I on my way to becoming an alcoholic, too?*

Tim was angry about all that had happened and grew increasingly withdrawn. Tim and I agreed to separate in 1999; he would keep James and I would keep Ryan. I found an apartment just three miles away.

Desperate to help Ryan, I took Social Services to court for them to accept custody of Ryan so I could get him the help he needed. Let me explain. In Virginia, at the time, parents of children with mental illness were forced to relinquish custody of their children to Social Services in order to get help—since the mental health departments lacked funding, the only avenue was Social Services. But Social Services wouldn't take mentally ill children unless they were abandoned, abused, or neglected. Ryan was loved and cared for—just very ill. I knew I had to go to court to fight for Ryan and do whatever it took. No matter how my heart was breaking, I knew this was the only course of action. The kind judge agreed and helped me.

Although the caseworker from Social Services was angry at first, we ended up getting along well. After much battling, Ryan went to an outdoor wilderness program when he was 12. He returned home eighteen months later and custody was returned to me. The program had helped, but his progress was hard to maintain. During that time, Tim and I had gotten back together, but it was too late. We both felt that we owed it to the kids to stay together and do all that we could to work things through. But the gulf had grown too wide and Ryan's unpredictable behavior put James at risk. Brotherly tussling could become dangerous due to the age gap and the physical disparity. Ryan was much bigger and stronger than James and didn't know his own strength. Tim and I separated permanently in 2001.

I bought a condo three miles from Tim's house and we managed to co-parent for the next five years. My life was full with the needs of my boys, working a full-time job and enrolling in a Ph.D. program in public policy.

As a result of all that Ryan and I had been through, I didn't want to see another parent have to relinquish custody of their child with a mental illness to get the help they needed as Virginia law required. I also wanted to help people, particularly at-risk kids, so I set up a nonprofit organization that was dedicated to improving the lives of kids with behavioral and learning challenges.

The focus was on a back-to-nature approach to healing, much like a Native American camp that stressed simple foods, simple life, simple spirituality, learning and living from the land. I thought having a Ph.D. would provide credibility and give me the tools I needed to find the correct answers to help these kids. But I learned that finding the truth on any particular topic was often a very complicated and difficult challenge that even the best minds could not always meet.

I had some great professors who touched my heart and showed me that the best and the brightest minds were often the most humble. Academia taught me that I really didn't know much at all and if I had been looking to find clarity, I had only opened the door to more doubt and ambiguity.

CHAPTER 3
THE MEETING

Curiosity made me go that night. And if I'm honest, Greg, too. He was a man I had met the year before when, concerned about my drinking, I'd gone to AA. I'd since stopped going because I was not sure if I met the criteria for alcoholism. I thought I could stop and stay stopped. I liked the program's tools and found the steps of recovery helpful for whatever issues I was facing, though, but I did not feel the need to continue going. However, my attitude changed when I tried drinking again and came to understand that I was, indeed, an alcoholic. I would never be able to drink safely. I had finally accepted it and had picked up a white chip of surrender on March 20th, 2005.

The past year I had been swamped with teaching, getting my nonprofit venture off the ground, and working on my Ph.D. dissertation. Even though I liked Greg, I had lost contact with him and other friends due to all of my other responsibilities.

We had reconnected when my former sponsor, Sandy, had asked me to come to the Richmond AA meeting where she was celebrating 20 years of sobriety. I saw Greg at that meeting and now he was calling. I was excited thinking that maybe he and I would have a chance to finally connect. We had danced around each other for quite a while with things not moving forward, though I wasn't sure why.

Our chats were mainly about his friend, David, who had some major health problems. I had helped Greg with health issues in the past and he knew I was always interested in discussing nutritional options. He also knew I worked with energy for healing, specifically Reiki, a Japanese method that I had demonstrated to him before. At first, I didn't know if he was hinting that it would be nice if I offered to help his friend out. Greg actually insisted that I already knew David. He thought we all must have met at an AA meeting at some point during the past year. But I hadn't been going so I felt sure we hadn't met there or anywhere else.

He told me too that David was having terrible ear infections that led to migraine headaches and now he had Bell's palsy, where David's face was partially paralyzed. He was growing sicker by the day and no physician could diagnose the problem. Greg was worried.

As the weeks went by, Greg called to let me know that David had been admitted to St. Mary's Hospital. Major organ systems had shut down, including complete lung and kidney failure. He had been placed on a ventilator to help him breathe and a dialysis machine to cleanse his blood. I told Greg I was sorry to hear what was happening and would keep his friend in my prayers.

When Greg called again that night he told me more. David had been in a coma for more than three weeks and was heading into his fourth week. The machines were barely keeping him alive. Greg said that David's family, who lived in San Francisco, had visited twice before and had been called today to come say goodbye. He said that David's mother, who was in AA, was going to be at the meeting that night at 7 PM.

"Would you like to meet me there? We plan to have a prayer session for David after the meeting."

I felt tired and had been pondering the class I had to teach the next day. Also, I planned to relax a little and watch one of my favorite shows, *Wheel of Fortune*. I hesitated.

Aside from my desire to see Greg and reconnect with my friends, I felt an inner urge that would not let me rest and instead prompted me to go. I clicked the TV off, slipped on my shoes, and ran out the door.

CHAPTER 4
MEETING MAMA DEE

Thursday, September 22, 2005

Sandy, my former sponsor, greeted me at the door. "Hey stranger! Good to see you!"

"Good to see you, too," I said, as we hugged. "So, you know David?"

"Yes."

"I've never met him."

"Scarlett, you've met David. Remember? He's got dark hair and glasses."

I shook my head. "Sandy, I don't know him. That could describe just about anyone. I don't think I ever met him. I haven't been here for nearly a year."

"Then what are you doing here?" Sandy laughed.

"Greg called and told me about what was going on and that people were going to pray for him. He thought it would be nice for me to come. Plus, he said David's mother was coming tonight."

Sandy rolled her eyes. She didn't feel Greg was good for me and made no bones about it.

There were several familiar faces milling around as well as some I did not recognize. I felt a tug of annoyance that Greg wasn't there.

I wandered off to say hello to Frank and some other friends I was surprised to see.

How did David know so many of my friends? Had I really been that out of the loop?

I was hugging another friend I hadn't seen in quite a while, Dan, when Sandy came over and nudged me. "There's David's mother," she said, pointing toward the front door. "She flew all the way from San Francisco today."

Sandy sighed, shaking her long, blonde hair out of her eyes. "Did you hear what happened, Scarlett?" She liked to say my name during our conversations. I'd gotten used to it mostly, although sometimes it seemed a little strange. It was a Southern thing, she had explained. Plus, using names was part of her sales training at her bakery job. Always use the customer's name—it increases sales. It really does, she had added, to be sure I was convinced.

"I heard she was going to be here and that David's doing very badly."

David's mother came into the room and everyone stopped talking. It was as if the group seemed to freeze. I could feel a pall throughout and shivered from the chill. I looked around at my friends, at their somber expressions.

Frank's green eyes were moist and Sheila was crying. Sheila didn't do anything quietly, so she was sniffling rather loudly. Sean, who was David's roommate, Sandy had informed me, was staring down at the floor. His throat was working, swallowing. Still, he wouldn't look up.

Nathan was shaking his head sadly. "It's a damn shame," I heard him mutter.

Greg came in late and he, too, seemed subdued. He stood near the door and nodded slightly in my direction, a rueful smile curving his thin lips slightly.

Dan, who was a close friend of Greg's, cleared his throat. "Hi everyone, thanks for coming." He stood over 6'4" and was full-bellied and broad-shouldered. He had played football in his youth and still carried himself with the easy lope of the athlete, even though he was now in his mid-sixties. Those extra pounds and knee problems didn't detract from his youthful looks. I had always liked him and considered him a kind man. Although he was usually cheerful, tonight sadness blanketed his face.

I glanced at Sandy, arching my eyebrow at her. What was going on? Had David died?

Dan cleared his throat twice more. I looked up and noticed his bright blue eyes filling with tears.

"I want to introduce you all to David's mom, Dee. She flew here from San Francisco and is leaving tomorrow. If you haven't heard by now, David took a turn for the worse today."

He paused. I glanced at Dee. She had soft gray hair, cut short; no make-up. She looked tired and drawn, lines of worry etched on her face. Wire-rimmed glasses framed her eyes.

Sheila sniffled loudly, her red curls springing like metal coils as her head bobbled toward the tissue she was clutching to her nose.

Dan continued: "You all know that David is on life support and dialysis, but the doctor said today that he's not doing well and the machines aren't accomplishing what they need to. David's brain is shutting down and it's not looking good ... Anyway, Dee wanted to say a few words, so I'll turn this over to her. Dee ..."

Everyone looked over at Dee. She took a deep breath and began to speak softly, her voice heavy with sorrow and resignation.

"Hello. I want to tell you how much I appreciate the love and support you have shown for David and his family. Most of you know David's story and you know that things have been really hard for him. He told me that this was the first time he felt he had found a home. I'm grateful he found sobriety. If he had to come all the way to the East Coast to find it, well, I can't thank you enough for that." She paused.

Everyone was looking at her, waiting. I racked my brain searching for any memory of meeting David somewhere along the line during that past year, but nothing came to mind.

"I can't tell you what it means to me to know that he finally found a place where he felt loved and cared for. A mother always wants that for her son and I know it had been lacking for him for a long time. Thank you for that."

Dee was obviously sad, but she also exuded a quiet acceptance and serenity. There was something about her that was very compelling. It was as if she was able to hold her strong feelings in check while expressing them honestly.

"The doctor told me today that they don't expect David to make it. That's why they called us to come today."

Sandy whispered in my ear that this was their third visit in three and a half weeks.

"When they called us to come, they told me that we needed to be prepared to say goodbye. They also needed to know the next steps and what we wanted regarding funeral arrangements. We are praying we'll have the chance to see David alive one more time before we go back home. Again, all of you, thanks." Dee's voice trailed off.

The room remained quiet. No one really knew what to say. Then someone muttered something, people began shuffling about, and a hint that the meeting should get started surfaced.

A Native American saying popped into my mind during that interlude: "It's a good day to die."

According to a book I had read earlier that day, this statement was made just before Indians went into battle. They accepted that life and death were intertwined and that the spirit lived on, so any day was a good day to leave life, which never ended anyway. They could accept their fate with quiet dignity.

I was working then on a part of my dissertation dealing with the state-recognized Virginia Indians' fight for federal recognition and so had been researching Indian history. I had Native American roots from my North Carolina side (Cherokee and Tuscarora, we had been told) and had been trying to trace my genealogy, so it was apt that Native American wisdom was top of mind. I spoke up.

"The Indians say that any day is a good day to die. Especially when you've lived a good life and have loved and been loved. I haven't met David, but he sounds like he is a really special person. I'm sorry to hear this sad news and I can see that he has touched a lot of people here." Dee nodded.

I realized she was a mother who loved her son as much as I loved my boys. Several people were openly crying now. Their sadness at David's impending death permeated the atmosphere. I thought he must be a pretty nice guy if all these people cared so much. I regretted how nonchalant I had been when Greg had told me about him. "Maybe it's his time to go," I'd said when Greg was telling me how fast David's health was deteriorating.

I had heard he was on everyone's prayer list. Churches across the country were praying for him and were continuing their prayers even now. Two of my friends, both of whom were powerful in working with energy healing, had told me they knew about David through Sheila and had been asked to pray for him. I didn't know how they knew Sheila, but the circles were closing in and David seemed to be at the center. Maybe I should have gone to visit or done something. But now it was too late.

All of a sudden, I could feel everyone's grief like a palpable force and it moved me deeply. I felt like I should do something to help. But what could I possibly do that would help him now? My mind swirled with thoughts and the emotional surge I had ignored for weeks was taking over.

As the meeting was drawing to an end, Dan led us in closing with the Lord's Prayer.

People were talking after the meeting and there were some snacks on the table, but no one ate. There was little more left to say that night. People soon began hugging and saying goodbye while others were putting the coffee pots away and doing a final clean-up of the room.

Greg came over to tell me he was too bummed out to get together after this. I wasn't really surprised.

"That's okay," I said. "Maybe we can catch up this weekend." He shrugged, non-committal as always.

I saw David's mother was getting ready to leave. Dan was saying something to her, giving her one of his giant bear hugs. All of a sudden, I felt a hand on my back, propelling me forward, towards them. I turned to see who was pushing me but there was no one.

Then, to my surprise, I was standing in front of Dee, face to face. I took her hand and held it in both of mine and looked into her warm, brown eyes filled with sadness. Something in my spirit recognized this woman and I knew I wanted to do whatever I could to ease her suffering. I felt connected to her in an inexplicable way.

"I don't think you should give up hope yet."

I couldn't believe the words that had just tumbled out of my mouth.

Dee just looked at me, her face expressionless at first and then shifting to slightly surprised. It was clear from what she had said earlier and the reactions of everyone else that it was too late, so she didn't quite know what to make of me. She must have thought I had failed to comprehend the severity of the situation. Obviously, it didn't make any sense for me to offer words of hope.

I had already told her how sorry I was to hear of David's plight and acknowledged her sadness and loss. Still, I didn't feel it was the truth of the situation, at least according to my own intuition. It often didn't matter how things appeared. The *knowing* had taken over and found its own still, small voice and it would not be denied.

By now I was at a crossroads: my rational mind was telling me I was out of line to tell her not to give up hope; my intuition was telling me that it was the right thing to say. I didn't trust either. I cleared my throat, frantically thinking about what I should say to back-pedal from that crazy statement while still respecting my intuitive sense.

"What I mean is, well, I could go visit your son if you'd like. I do energy work and it might help him. Are you familiar with Reiki?"

"Well, yes," answered Dee. She paused. "But he's Jewish."

"I figured that with a name like Schwartz," I laughed.

She smiled for the first time that night.

"Don't worry, Reiki doesn't interfere with anyone's religion. It's a universal life force energy. It's very gentle and soothing. It won't do any harm. It's kind of like this—here, I'll show you. Just open your hand and hold it out next to mine."

She held out her hand and I encased it with both of mine hovering around but not touching. The energy and heat began to flow immediately and I could feel the tingles radiate from my hands to hers.

"Do you feel that?"

"Yes," she said, nodding her head.

"I can't guarantee anything and I can't promise anything, but I feel this might at the very least provide some comfort to David. Would you like me to try?"

Dee looked at me, considering... then finally, "Okay."

I knew she didn't believe that anything could help, but she could feel my sincerity and I guess she figured that it couldn't do any harm at this point.

"I'll go see him tomorrow after I finish teaching my class. It ends at one, so I'll head over then. Won't you need to add my name to the visitors list? I don't think they'll let me visit without your permission."

Neither one of us openly acknowledged that he might not be around for a visit. That possibility, probability, hung unspoken between us.

I reached into my purse, grabbed my business card and handed it to her.

"I'll let them know to add your name," she said.

I smiled warmly and gave her a quick hug. I left, feeling unsettled, anxious, and second-guessing why I had ever offered to go visit her son.

I drove home in a blur, my mind swirling with agitated thoughts.

I didn't know David and I sure didn't have time for any of this. In addition to working on my Ph.D. dissertation and being a graduate teaching assistant, I was also an adjunct professor teaching a Social Science course entitled Marriage and Family Relationships three days a week. I'd gotten the chance to teach the class because I told the hiring professor that I'd made just about every mistake in relationships humanly possible so I'd be in a perfect position to tell students what *not* to do.

After he finished laughing, he hired me. I was also a graduate teaching assistant two days a week for two criminal justice courses. None of this paid beans and I was wondering how I was going to put gas in my car to make it through another week.

My oldest son, Ryan, was struggling in his special education classes. He was 17 and in the tenth grade, challenged with severe learning disabilities and ADHD. I was supposed to go for a conference later that week to see if there was any chance he would be able to finish high school. My youngest, James, was 10 and had epilepsy. Managing the boys' needs was often overwhelming.

The last thing I needed was to take on one more task. A visit to someone I didn't even know seemed senseless. During the past few years, I had gone on healing visits for people who were in crisis, but those were people I knew and cared about. David was a stranger to me.

Yet, somehow this time felt different. I didn't know whether or not there was anything I could do to help, but at least I could pray with David as he hovered between life and death.

I had done that for my father when his last heart attack left him barely alive and on a ventilator. He had been pronounced brain dead, having been revived after a seemingly eternal 45 minutes on the cusp of "the other side," and was lingering in the hospital Intensive Care Unit for the few hours it took me to get there. I knew he had waited for me to get to the hospital to say goodbye.

Those final moments with my father had been a moving experience that opened portals to divine love and forgiveness. My heart felt compassion and sorrow for him and I wanted him to be healed for all that he had suffered in his life. I could feel his pain and his need to be forgiven. The forgiveness I felt was so enormous that there was no trace of resentment, only love. I could see that he had suffered from untreated depression and trauma from his youth that had contributed to his displaced rage. I saw that he was a fragile human being who had made mistakes. I also remembered that he had tried hard to overcome those issues in later life by getting an education, trying to be supportive of us as he got older, and helping others in life. He had made his amends and now it was time for him to go in loving peace.

I knew I could access that loving force and help David cross over, if needed, just as I had with my dad. Unbeknownst to me, within days, I would personally experience a peek behind a curtain that would alter the course of my life and my sense of reality as I had known it.

CHAPTER 5

FIRST VISIT

Friday, September 23, 2005

A sense of urgency jarred me awake that morning. The thought went through my mind that if I didn't get to the hospital soon it would be too late.

I called ahead to see if my name had been added to the visitor's list. It had not. Feeling a clutch of anxiety, I asked if David's mother was there so she could give permission.

"She left this morning to go back to California," the nurse replied. I was puzzled why she would have left. Later I found out that she had just been diagnosed with a major health condition and was having some serious side effects from the recent medications. And, she had made peace with David's impending passing.

Since I didn't have Dee's phone number, I asked the nurse if she would call her and ensure that my name was added because I intended to visit David at around 1:30 p.m.

I was teaching at noon and figured I would go after class but then debated whether to go to the hospital before class. While I had been resisting the urge to go see David for the past several weeks from my conversations with Greg, after I'd met Mama Dee the night before, I now felt an overwhelming urgency as though I was being drawn beyond my control.

The conflicting emotions were confusing, but at least now I was listening to the nudging of my intuition, which was not going to let up until I saw him. After struggling with it all, I decided to stay committed to teaching my class and pray that he would hang on until afterwards.

I got to class early. It was only one hour long but there were more than 120 students in the lecture hall for that day's topic on the many forms that relationships can take. I let the students out a little early anyway. It was Friday, so they were happy.

I sped to the hospital, praying the entire way. It took me about 20 minutes to get there. David was in the Cardiac Care Unit. I pressed the buzzer. A nurse approached and opened the door.

I introduced myself and told her I was there to see David. The nurse informed me she would have to check my name against the visitors list.

I explained I had called earlier to make sure his mom had been contacted so that I would be added.

She disappeared to go check and I stood there, wondering whether or not my visit would work out. I would take it as a sign from God either way. Just then, she returned. "Your name has been added to the list. You may come in."

So there I was to provide David with what comfort I could—and soothe my own nagging intuitive voice that wouldn't let me rest. My mind raced from one thought to another as I followed the nurse to his room.

I'd been a fan of paranormal studies ever since I was old enough to talk and had been an avid researcher into all things weird, especially wanting to make sense of my experiences. As a child, out-of-body experiences were a frequent occurrence for me. Curiosity about reincarnation, the ability to predict events before they happened, such as my best friend's parents' divorce when we were eight, were normal for me.

When I was 16, my Aunt Marian called me on our old black rotary phone in the middle of the day to ask me to tell my mother to stop grieving. Aunt Marian had died a few months before and Mom was having a hard time dealing with her sister's loss. I had received visits from her two other times after her death. The first time was within days of her death. She appeared at my bedside and she looked like she was decaying. I was terrified. But her message was for me to tell my mother to stop grieving and that she was okay. The next time I was waking up from a dream about her and she was there again at my bedside. This time, she was glowing radiantly and looked beautiful. Her message was the same: tell your mother to please stop grieving. I had no idea that dead people could use something as mundane as a phone. Her disembodied voice, repeating the message to tell my mother to stop grieving, crackling over the static totally freaked me out. I dropped the phone and ran outside. I had never heard of this in 1975 and it wasn't until about 30 years later that I found out this had happened to many people more than was commonly known.

The *knowing*, as I called it, was always accompanied by a desire to do something good. The overriding theme was to help and to heal. I always liked to comfort and soothe people in distress—it was an innate ability. Throughout the years, I continued to study consciousness, paranormal abilities, and healing modalities. Even in my mainstream academic setting, I was challenged to present an innovative approach to solving world issues as part of an Organizational Dynamics class in my PhD program. Based on my paper, I was invited by my classmates from Turkey to present my research in Istanbul in June 2005, at the first world conference on

SCARLETT L. HEINBUCH, PhD

Anti-Terrorism and World Peace,[1] hypothesizing that a higher consciousness was a reliable path to healing and evolving as humans. I talked about developing the sixth sense as a normal next-step developmental tool for human evolution.

I had presented research about near-death experiences (University of Virginia), out-of-body experiences (Monroe Institute), extrasensory perception (Duke), remote viewing (Stanford), and reincarnation (UVA). I had removed the reincarnation information at the Istanbul conference, though, because the sponsors discouraged it. I expounded instead on the ability of the sixth sense to be used as a healing form that transcended time and space which could tap into the wellspring of Source through the magnetized energy of the power of an ever-abiding, all-encompassing, indescribable, liquid-light love. I could feel the truth of this liquid-light love in my bones. I'd had experiences and glimpses into another dimension that elevated me and reminded me that there was something so wonderful and huge that if we could just harness a molecule of it, we'd all be better off. I knew it. I'd researched it. I felt it. And I had previously worked with it. Now would it help with David?

The nurse led me down the hall to David's hospital room. The lights were off and the room was eerily illuminated by greenish lights from the life support machines and monitors glowing through the door's window.

Upon entering, I stood still, absorbing the energies in the room. I stared at David's face, but the tubes and the

---

[1] Heinbuch (Bowes), Scarlett L., Toward a Higher Consciousness for World Peace: The Development of the Sixth Sense. First International Conference on Anti-Terrorism & World Peace. Istanbul, Turkey, June 2005.

excessive bloating made it impossible to see what he looked like. I didn't recognize him and felt certain we had not met before, even though some of my friends thought we had. If so, it had not been in this lifetime—that much I knew. But that was the only thing I could be certain of in the moment.

I knew in my heart that all events were converging to bring me to this point. I also trusted God to guide me in all things. So, I reasoned, *I must be in the exact intended place.* That didn't mean I knew what to do. Actually, I felt divided in two as though I was observing both of us from a distance while also experiencing awareness of the present moment. My mind was telling me that it was too late, but my spirit had a drive of its own.

I remembered that my mother, a career nurse, told me that patients in a coma could hear every word spoken in the room, so it was important to be very careful what you say in their presence. Since David and I had not met, it seemed the next logical step was to introduce myself just like I would if we were meeting for the first time.

I moved closer, standing on the right side of the bed.

His eyes were closed. His lids were still. He was so close to death that the machines keeping him alive were giving off more energy than he was; yet I was determined to talk to him as though he were conscious. That approach seemed more respectful. But I also knew he was in an altered state of consciousness and that if healing were to occur, there was no time to mince words. I had to get to the heart of the matter quickly. I knew my intuition would reveal the way, if he was willing to allow the connection. He really was in charge, more than he knew.

"Hi David," I began. "You don't know me, but my name is Scarlett and I'm friends with your friends: Frank, Sandy, Dan, Greg, and Sheila. I met your mom last night. I told her that I work with a type of energy healing called Reiki. I offered to visit and see if I could help you. Is that okay? I'm here because a lot of people love you and that tells me you must be a pretty nice guy."

I paused as the machines continued to beep and the ventilator continued to breathe in that steady, unnatural rhythm.

"I know you must be feeling really vulnerable right now and that it seems like you have no control over anything. But you do. You have control over giving me permission to work with you. I will not do anything without your permission. Okay? I know you can't respond in ordinary ways right now, but I can hear you with my mind if you want to send a thought to me. While you think about it, I'd like to tell you a little bit about Reiki, just so you know what it is. Your mom said you're Jewish so I wanted you to know that Reiki is not a religious form of energy. It's a Japanese system of aligning your body, mind, and spiritual energy into harmony. If I need to touch you, I'll ask you first and wait for you to let me know with your mind if it's okay before I go ahead. That's the way it works with you in control."

I felt a shift in the room as a light breeze swept over me. I checked that the door was still closed. I was keeping my voice soft and low, but strong. I could feel that it was fine to proceed.

I asked his permission to hold his hand, the one with the pulse oximeter monitor clipped on his index finger and a taped IV line on the back of his hand. I waited for him to signal his consent and again felt the subtle breeze. I gently took his hand in both of mine.

I wasn't sure what I was picking up, but I sensed some static and friction as though he was upset that I had not come sooner. How could he be mad at me? But that's how it felt. Had the nagging intuition I'd felt been his spirit calling to me for help? Why me? He didn't know me, so why would he want me to come? It didn't make sense and I thought I must be misinterpreting this... this... whatever it was. Even so, I figured it couldn't hurt to make amends.

"I feel like I owe you an apology. I know I should have come before now and I'm sorry I took so long to get here. I'll do my best to make it up to you." I could feel the energy shift as though he accepted my apology. How odd, I thought, but he seemed to have calmed down.

"Would you like me to get started?" I waited, my hands still holding his. There was no grip in his fingers, which were also terribly swollen. I shifted my foot and accidentally bumped the rail very slightly. His entire body shook like gelatin. I had never seen anyone in acute kidney failure and didn't realize at the time that his body was unable to excrete fluids, leading to swollenness and toxicity. Instead of being repulsed though, I felt compassion and sorrow.

I could feel his approval and took a deep breath. "Thank you. I'm glad you'd like me to work with you. Let's get started." My voice sounded unfamiliar—it was soft and slow and very soothing. Normally, I talked fast because I had learned to do so with an ADHD child and also because my students tuned out quickly if I didn't hold their attention. Now, I lowered my pitch. I was beginning to feel very still inside and could also feel myself attuning to David even more keenly.

I began to synchronize my breathing with the machine, which was the same as synchronizing with him. The machine forced me to slow down and breathe in a measured way. When my breathing pattern matched his, I began the treatment.

I placed my right hand on his forehead to make the connection. That's when the feeling of overwhelming love and compassion flooded into my soul. Something ancient and primal had been stirred within me as tears welled in my eyes. He looked so innocent and yet I was flooded with strong feelings of pain, confusion, and grief. I felt echoes of a barrage of emotions rushing into my body and mind. I sensed all the fear, the wrong choices, the sorrows, how lost he had become. It all swirled around like a dust cloud in a dark valley, which is where I perceived he was. How had this happened to him? What had brought him to this? A feeling of intense sorrow enveloped me.

I began the energy assessment scans; lightly scanning his body by hovering my hands from the top of his head, around his side, over his chest, down to his feet and back up again. His body energy was barely perceptible. But I could feel the healing energy begin to flow through my hands.

"I know you've heard people talking in the room about how bad things look for you right now. But I'm here because I see things in a different way from most people. I believe in miracles, David, because I've had them happen in my life and I know they're real. The God of my understanding is a miracle-working God. I know that it's true and so I don't believe for one second that it's too late for you. And neither should you."

I felt my heart open and the loving compassion in my spirit begin to spin like a wheel. I could sense the raw pain of his emotions. On the other hand, the love force that was now flowing focused with equal rawness on his innocent spirit. The connection was made and we were communicating. He was listening.

"I don't care what you've done, who you've hurt, or what you are feeling so guilty over that you feel you can't go on. The only thing I see, David, is your innocence. There are many people who love you. Do you know that? I believe if

so many people love you then you might have some unfinished business and you may need to stick around. Don't you
know how many people love you and need you? Frank has
been coming every day to be here with you. No matter what
you may have done, God has already forgiven you. There is
nothing that God hasn't already forgiven and God can heal
you right now, if you want to be healed. Can you feel that
love enfolding you? I can."

I stopped talking. I could feel the energy building
around him and surrounding me, too. It was the living presence of love encircling us both.

"You've got to know that there is so much love around
you right now. God's love is ever-present with you. The love
and prayers of the many who are praying for you encompass
you right now like a beautiful blanket of shimmering light.
Breathe it in, David, the awesome power of love. I see the
healing white light of love. It flows around you, showering
you with love, peace, forgiveness, and acceptance. I can feel
the power and presence of living love shining on you. You
are God's child and no one has the right to judge you, not
even you. I know that your soul pattern is being worked out
by you and God. Do you feel it?"

I was receiving information very clearly letting me know
he understood it was his choice whether to stay in this life
or to leave it. He was mainly gone and it appeared he had
made his choice. Still, something was holding him here in
that swollen body.

"I know you have to choose whether to leave this life or
to stay." I paused. He really was in charge.

"Whatever you choose to do will be fine. If you want to go
to the light and to that love, then go in peace, knowing that
you are loved and forgiven. If that makes sense and you're
really done with this life, then go. But it seems to me with all

these people who love you, you might have some unfinished business. And I know I'm here for a reason. So, if you and God decide you're not done and you want to come back, I'll make a promise to you. I'll see you through this. I don't know why I'm making this promise, but I am and I keep my word."

As the words poured from my mouth, I knew this was a sacred time and I was inserting myself in the middle of it.

When I finished the treatment, I scanned his body as though I were zipping up an invisible suit that would seal him energetically. The whole session took about 25 minutes. Nurse Sherry had poked her head in so I knew it was time to go. As I was preparing to leave, I took his hand one more time to say a prayer of thanks and gratitude for this healing time and to remind him that I would continue coming if he decided he wanted to stick around.

His hand was limp—he had no ability to move his fingers or respond. As I began to pull my hand away though I was surprised to find I couldn't move it. His open palm felt like it was seamed to mine. I pulled a little, but what I believed was a magnetic force kept my hand pressed to his. I knew if I yanked hard I might break the connection. But why would I do that when he wasn't ready to release my presence with him? He was reaching back energetically and I needed to be present with him in that moment.

I smiled.

"Oh, so you don't want me to leave? Well, okay. I'll stay here a bit longer."

I stood beside his bed, our hands pressed together, listening to the machines and looking at the rainbow of bright lights—red, purple, yellow, green—splashing forth data from the heart monitor, glowing like beacons.

I silently prayed that God would heal every organ in his body if he chose to come back to this life. Otherwise, he would return to a body that was permanently disabled. It wasn't up to me to judge that outcome, but it sure didn't sound like it would be much fun. I glanced at his wristband and saw that his birthday was in December. He would be 43 in a few months, if he lived. After about five minutes, the energy left—poof—it was just gone.

I knew it was time to go. After telling him that I would be back, I gave his hand a final squeeze and left.

I headed home in a blur, feeling the aftereffects of the healing energy, which rarely happened to this degree. I did know that I was moved beyond anything I'd felt before. When I got home (my condo was just across the bridge, only about 15 minutes away from the hospital), I immediately sat down and prayed. Then I fell into a deep sleep and didn't wake up until nearly time for dinner.

Later that night I was thinking more about what had happened. If he really did stick around, I knew I would have to as well; almost as though I had signed on the dotted line of a legally binding spiritual contract and now had to adhere to it. There was a bond and that was that.

I had worked with many sick, vulnerable people—male and female. In all cases, I was able to tap into that source of universal love and consciousness to varying degrees, depending on the person and the condition they were experiencing. That universal love felt generic; it was the power of love, but it wasn't personal, which meant that mainly I did the healing work and moved on, always grateful when my clients improved and accepting even when they didn't. I respected a person's inner wisdom and knew that dying, like recovering, was a form of healing too.

I also wasn't one to get attached to my clients. It wasn't emotionally healthy, it wasn't in the healer's ethical code, and quite honestly, I wasn't attracted to sick people. Since I had never developed those attachments, I did not anticipate the feeling of devotion that would rise up in the coming days.

As I drifted off to sleep, I kept David in my prayers and visualized myself in his room continuing the healing as we slept, wondering too if he would choose to live or die. Later that night, I woke up and felt David's presence in my bedroom. Had he died and come to say goodbye? I felt a sense of loving peace and went back to sleep.

Chapter 6

The Cord of Connection

Saturday, September 24, 2005

It was Saturday and I had promised James a fun day. Ryan had gotten a part-time job at a restaurant and had biked to work.

We planned to attend the 54th Annual Chickahominy Indian Tribe Fall Festival and Powwow in Charles City. I was involved with the Virginia Indians largely through writing my dissertation on the quest for official federal tribal acknowledgment that six of the eight state-recognized tribes sought. Plus, my family had Native American roots—although not with the Virginia Indians—and I felt it important for the boys to stay connected to that part of their ancestral history.

I was torn. I also wanted to see David and didn't know how I could squeeze both into one day.

I called the hospital to determine David's condition, half-expecting to hear that he had passed on. A part of me knew that I should not be attached to the outcome of David's choice while another part of me was not ready to hear that he had declined to stay.

"David's condition is unchanged," the nurse told me. I didn't expect the feeling of elation that swept over me when I heard he was hanging onto this life.

"That's great news to hear. I'll be by later," I said. A part of me wanted to go right then, but I had first promised today to James and we both were looking forward to the adventure. But before we left I spent some quiet time in prayer for David's continued healing. I felt a connection—almost as though he could hear me. It was like speaking into an echoing tube with my words and emotions carried on a stream of light directly to him.

James and I enjoyed our time at the powwow. I saw several friends from various tribes and introduced my son to them. He had planned to return to his dad's that afternoon at around three, so I began thinking about David again. Earlier in the week I had arranged to have dinner with a classmate, Jackie, to talk about school and spiritual things. But that was before I had met David's mom and gone to see him. Now, I couldn't wait to get Jackie's view on all that had occurred. She is very metaphysically oriented and was guiding me with my visualizations to attract my twin flame. Both of us thought it was Greg. We excused his lack of attentiveness by rationalizing he just had not yet caught on to the attraction but would soon enough, we were sure.

After I dropped James off at his dad's, I headed to the hospital.

As busy as the hospital was, the atmosphere seemed quiet and subdued; the prevailing sense of order calmed me. I walked to the elevator and pressed the button. Alone on the slow elevator, I thought about David and wondered how he was doing—my thoughts interrupted by the ding the elevator made each time we passed a floor.

When the doors opened, I turned to the left and headed to the Cardiac Care Unit (CCU). I was surprised to see the CCU doors open, and while I hesitated briefly, I went on in.

I stopped by the nurse's desk to let her know I was there to see David.

"How's he doing now?" I asked Nurse Sherrie.

"He seems about the same." She looked at me appraisingly, searching for a clue as to whether or not I was trustworthy. She was clearly protective of her patient, something I was glad to see. David was in a vulnerable state and I was a stranger, so it was really good to know that he had someone watching out for him. "He's had a few visitors today to keep him company but they've all headed out so this is good timing," she said.

"I'm here to do Reiki with him again," I explained with a smile. She nodded her head and told me I could go on in. I heard her drag her chair over and station herself outside the room, just like she had the day before.

The room was dark, except for the glow of the machines. Nurse Sherrie was right—David seemed the same. His eyes were closed, the machine was still breathing for him, and all the monitors, tubes, and bags were exactly as they had been the day before, hanging in their respective positions. I walked toward the bed.

"Hi, David. It's Scarlett. You're still here and I came back, just like I said I would. A deal's a deal, right?" I laughed softly. David's heart monitor began beeping faster. I looked up and noticed his heart rate had increased. He was aware of my presence, even though he was still unresponsive. That was a good sign.

"Ready to get started? Today I'm going to use the same techniques I did yesterday. Okay? First, I'd like to start with a prayer of thanks to God for this healing time together."

Carefully, I reached for his hand and held it in mine. I placed my index finger on the spot between his eyebrows, often referred to as the "third eye." I began to pray quietly, but loud enough for David to hear my words. I thanked God for David's life, his healing and recovery, and expressed gratitude for the opportunity to serve God and my fellow traveler as a channel for healing energies.

I barely had time to declare *Amen* when the healing energy zoomed into and through me. In a flash, my hands were red hot, magnetic waves radiating from my fingers and palms. The vibrational buzz began instantly and my hands started scanning David's body. I was drawn to his kidney area, where my hands hovered for about two minutes. The rest of my body though was unable to move; it felt as if my feet were cemented to the floor. I stood still, allowing the energy to flow through, trying to stay focused and centered. Then my body began experiencing a kind of floating sensation when energy is flowing full-tilt.

I was pleased that the energy moved so strongly today as it was clear David had made the choice to open himself to receive it. I knew it could not flow with such strength unless he had chosen to allow it.

Spiritual healing for me is a reciprocal process involving both healer and "healee," in which the two become one during the healing session. And for that period of time, David and I became one. Because he was so critically ill, I knew it was important for me to remain centered so that the energy exchange circulated unfettered and didn't get snagged somehow in my energy field.

The energy seemed to have a vision of its own and it was now guiding my hands over his lungs. I went along, letting the energy take the lead. I truly felt as though I was simply serving as a conduit—with some other force guiding and controlling the energy, I simply had to let it flow through me. I was simultaneously a spectator observing the healing session, and the healer perceiving a total connection to David. It was an odd sensation to participate and be present with the energy while at the same time feeling that I was outside of myself, observing it all.

The energy seemed to finish what it had set out to do and then was gone as quickly as it had appeared. I stood still, slightly dazed. I realized I was a little chilled and my clothes were damp. I had gotten so hot that I was sweating, dampening my clothes. My heart was racing; I felt like I had sprinted around the room. I was used to getting hot when I worked with people but I wasn't used to my heart pounding.

I took some deep breaths and looked at David's face. While he didn't look different, I intuited a shift in his energy. He seemed more peaceful, and his cheeks, which had been a pallid gray, were now slightly flushed. The machine continued its rhythmic breathing. I reached out to hold his hand almost as a ritual that seemed to be how we began and ended our sessions, then told him I would come to see him tomorrow if he still wanted me to.

"Thank you for our time today," I whispered. "Hang in there, okay?"

I turned to go. David's heart monitor began to increase its beeping. I took that as a signal that he heard me.

I was surprised to see Nurse Sherrie's chair empty. I guess she wasn't so worried about me anymore.

I had a few hours until Jackie and I were scheduled to meet for dinner. Once I put the groceries away, I felt zapped and so decided to take a short nap. I set the timer on the oven clock for one hour, headed for the couch, pulled the fleecy throw over me, and fell into a deep sleep. It seemed like only a few minutes had passed before the timer beeped that my hour was up.

Jackie and I met for dinner at our favorite Mexican restaurant. I told her about the huge connection with David and what had happened with the energies. She assured me that she, too, sensed something powerful and reminded me to trust my intuition.

I expressed my surprise about how deep this connection seemed to be. Jackie waved a dismissive hand at me.

"Oh, it's some karma stuff. You'll see. Just go help the poor man."

Jackie's down-to-earth wisdom always made me laugh.

Later that night, I woke up around 2:30 AM. I could feel David's presence in my room as though his eyes were looking at me. The intense connection between us was huge. I knew he was asking me to visit him again. I telepathically answered that I would come to see him later that day and encouraged him to rest now. I assured him that I would keep my promise.

I felt that he was connected to me; that we two were connected as a unit by a cord of the Source. Oddly enough, I felt strengthened by the connection rather than drained.

I'd had people try to connect to me energetically in the past, but I had always immediately struggled to disentangle, feeling drained and trapped. But not this time. Instead, I sighed contentedly, knowing that the strength of the connection would see him through to healing. That is, if he decided to stay.

CHAPTER 7
DAVID'S CHOICE

Sunday, September 25, 2005

I took a belly dancing class at noon on Sundays. Normally I enjoyed the lesson, which I shared with a friend, but today I couldn't wait for it to end. That's because before leaving home for it, I had called the hospital to see if... yes, to make sure David was still alive.

Changing clothes quickly after class, I got to the hospital soon after 1 p.m. I rushed up to his room anxious to see for myself how he was doing. Today, a different nurse was attending to David. She introduced herself as Anne and then I explained that I had come to do Reiki. She said that she had already been informed I would be visiting.

"How is he doing today?" I asked her.

"Well, something must be working," she said as we entered the room. "Look at that." She pointed to the catheter bag which now had something in it. "He started producing urine this morning."

She continued with just enough enthusiasm to sound truly excited. "This is a big deal. His kidneys are beginning to do their job."

As I approached the bed, I felt a flash of disappointment upon seeing he was still on the ventilator and still appeared unresponsive. However, when I took his hand, there was a slight response. At least I thought I saw his eyelids flicker.

I shared with David how happy I was to see he had chosen to stay for now and what a great job his body was doing in healing itself. I told him how well his kidneys were improving and asked him if he had heard what Nurse Anne said.

David's slight improvement had obviously encouraged the staff as they now seemed more accepting of my visits. "I'll be outside if you need anything," the nurse said as she left the room.

I resumed speaking to David, gently taking his hand. I told him of all the love and prayers that were continuing for him. I told him about the many cards that were taped to the wall and sitting on the window sill in his room. I told him about the poster on the wall about Jeans Day for David from his work, to raise money for his family's travel from the West Coast. I pointed out that while I was the one who could channel all that love along with the Reiki energy, he was the one doing the healing. Also, I said that I was the facilitator—the one who could help him reconnect to his inner energy source so together we would connect to all that was sacred, holy, and divine. That the universal life force, which is the essence of Reiki, was the energy that would assist his body to heal. However, he was truly in charge. I wanted to guide him into feeling empowered and understanding that he was not helpless, no matter how serious his condition appeared.

Then I began the treatment and almost immediately the energy in my body was elevated as if I had plugged into an electrical socket. I felt my inner being floating in midair. The energy swirled and circled around me, through me, around David, and through him like we were in an electrified cocoon together.

My entire body was on fire from the healing energy pouring out of every pore. I was sweating and my body was trembling head to toe from the current. Although David's eyes were closed, I could sense he was feeling the force swirling through us both too. The energy was cycling through us in a figure-eight pattern, weaving us together. This was a totally unique experience. We were connected together— one body. As our one body maintained the connection, we were also linked to a third component, a pulsing force field of liquid light—love. I could feel this triangulation flowing through our physical hands, then reaching out to his spirit.

I finished the session and praised David. "I'm amazed at how well you are working with the energy, powerfully absorbing it and circulating it." He was fighting for his life now and I knew I wanted to be there to help him come back. "You've got to keep fighting. I'll help you every step of the way, but you have to take to heart that this is your recovery."

I felt a strong sense of dedication and devotion to David. And for whatever reason my promise to him was what kept springing to my mind. I found myself committed to a someone I did not know. Intuitively I was certain of the call to work with him—that somehow I owed him this on some very deep level and was happy to have the privilege to serve.

Through the years, I had come to understand how we accumulate karma. I had also experienced déjà vu and intuitive flashes relating to my past lives. However, at that moment I was not feeling that he and I had been together before. Perhaps I was fulfilling a karmic debt that had not yet been revealed to me. Though I was puzzled over the loving attentiveness with which I worked with David, at the same time I knew it was where I needed to be.

Something in me was awakening. From within my core being, an awareness that I did actually know him was beginning to emerge, yet it still remained buried too deeply for me to comprehend. What I did understand, though still tentative, knowing he could change his mind, was that it seemed he was now choosing to live. And that I wanted him to live too.

CHAPTER 8
ENCOUNTER ON THE
OTHER SIDE

Monday, September 26, 2005

The Marriage and Family class I taught met at noon on Mondays, Wednesdays, and Fridays in a lecture hall with an enrollment of 120 students. Even though the class was large, student participation was good and I often felt I was learning more than I was teaching. Today's topic was marital happiness and how the partners we choose can impact every area of our lives, including our health, our finances, and our wellbeing. We also discussed why people married: for love, partnership, economic security, cultural pressure, loneliness, peer pressure, or to have children, among other reasons. And we talked about how understanding one's personal values is essential in deciding on the type of marriage or relationship desired.

When I had taken the class as a student ten years before, the professor had asked a key question. What kind of marriage would you choose: Marriage A or Marriage B?

"Marriage A" would be a lifelong marriage of about 45 to 50 years. Not great, but okay. You would have children, and while you weren't truly happy, you weren't truly miserable either. It would just be humdrum.

"Marriage B" would be an exhilarating union that was deeply fulfilling on every level—spiritually, emotionally, mentally, and physically. But there was a catch. You would only get ten years together. At the end of the ten years, your partner would die.

In answer to the professor's question I was surprised to see that most of my classmates raised their hands for Marriage A. I thought that everyone would want the incredible relationship, which is the one I chose. But that very point is what gave me the most insight. Most people would opt for mediocre and enduring rather than amazing but relatively brief. They would rather not be alone, even if the relationship was not particularly great. They would settle.

I asked my class this question today, with the same choices. There were other choices people could make, but for the sake of this exercise, we would use these examples to help students determine what matters to them in a relationship. This time, the majority of students chose Marriage B. I related the choices students made ten years ago and asked: "Why would you choose to be happy rather than settle for mediocrity?"

One of my students, Darius, who was usually quiet but always had something thoughtful to say when he did speak, raised his hand. "I guess I'd rather be with my soul mate even if we only get ten years than be with the wrong person for a really long time."

The rest of the class nodded their heads in agreement. It seemed I had a room full of romantics who believed in love and did not want to settle. Things had changed.

After class, I went to visit David. I arrived around 1:30 pm. Before going to his room, I chatted with Nurse Anne about how David was doing. She had been working with him since he entered the Cardiac Care Unit and decided to give me the whole story, as far as she knew it. Now it seemed she was accepting me as a member of the healing team as she disclosed a portion of David's medical background.

He was admitted to the hospital because he came to the emergency room thinking he was having a panic attack. He could not catch his breath. Actually, he was going into respiratory failure. Because his heart was racing, the doctors also suspected pericarditis, an inflammation of the heart lining. The admitting doctor diagnosed him with double pneumonia and ordered a lab to check for Legionnaire's disease. Within 24 hours his lungs had shut down and he was placed on a ventilator to keep him alive. By the time the lab results came back negative, his kidneys were starting to fail too. Over the next week and a half, thirteen medical specialists were called in to consult on his case.

No one knew what was happening to cause these systemic failures. They knew David had a massive ear infection and that he had already been scheduled to have surgery for mastoiditis (an inflammation in a portion of the bone in the skull behind the ear). Tubes had been placed in his ears due to the infection and he was taking numerous antibiotics. Still, he was steadily getting worse.

Finally, during the second week of David's hospital stay, a doctor suspected that he had a rare form of vasculitis, called Wegener's Granulomatosis[2].

With only about 500 cases diagnosed a year, it was easy to understand why it had not been quickly identified. The doctor who suspected it immediately ordered a biopsy of his

---

[2]   https://www.hopkinsvasculitis.org/types-vasculitis/wegeners-granulomatosis/

lung to check the Anti-neutrophil cytoplasmic antibodies (ANCA) level, which is often a key indicator of Wegener's. It initially came back negative, but when another biopsy was done, it came back positive. The first symptoms of Wegener's are recurring ear infections, nosebleeds, sinus problems, and headaches, all of which David had experienced. Also, the week before he entered the hospital, he had reported extreme joint stiffness and pain that was so debilitating he could not get out of bed. These symptoms were precursors to the illness entering its next stage.

Nurse Anne said that Wegener's Granulomatosis causes inflammation of the blood vessels, which in turn restricts blood flow to various organs, especially the kidneys, lungs, and upper respiratory tract. The restricted blood flow to these organs can cause damage to them or even their complete failure. In addition to the inflamed blood vessels, Wegener's produces a special type of inflammatory tissue—granulo-mas—found around the blood vessels. These granulomas can also destroy the surrounding normal tissue. The causes for Wegener's are unknown. What is known is that it is nei-ther an already identified infection nor is it a type of cancer, although anti-cancer medications, along with steroids are the usual treatment approach. Wegener's Granulomatosis is now known as Granulomatosis with Polyangiitis (GPA).

Early diagnosis and treatment of the condition can lead to a full recovery, but without treatment, it is fatal, usually from kidney failure. In David's case, he was already in acute kidney failure along with respiratory failure. He had a dial-ysis treatment scheduled for the next day, but now blood clots had formed.

The doctors had given him a blood thinner, but he had had an allergic reaction. Because he was at risk for a stroke, they next placed him on another blood thinner to help

diffuse the clots. For whatever reason, he was not respond-
ing to the treatment protocol for Wegener's. His heart had
gone into several bouts of atrial fibrillation, an irregular
heart rhythm. Instead of contracting the way it should, his
heart was quivering, and that placed him at greater risk for
cardiac arrest or a stroke or both.

Adding to the complications was David having been
further diagnosed with encephalopathy, which meant his
brain wasn't functioning—the doctors were concerned
that his brain was getting ready to shut down. Nurse Anne
explained that treating the underlying cause of the disorder may improve symptoms, but the encephalopathy may
cause irreversible damage to the brain. Some encephalopa-
thies can be fatal by themselves, let alone with everything
else going on, she said.

Also, because the only food he could ingest was through
a feeding tube in his nose, he was anemic and malnourished
too. His mouth held the tube for the ventilator. There was a
chest tube as well, because one of his lungs had collapsed.

Anne said that even with the new correct diagnosis and
the subsequent available treatment protocol having been
administered for the past two weeks, he was getting worse.
The odds were nearly impossible that he would survive at
this late stage. And if he did, he would be permanently
disabled due to the extensive kidney damage that had
occurred. He would be on dialysis for the rest of his life and
might never recover normal breathing functions. "And we
don't know what level of brain damage he might be facing if
he pulls through. But despite his dire condition, he started
to produce more urine again this morning, which indicates
some kind of improvement."

I thanked her for the information and assured her
that I was there to do what I could to help. Her demeanor

conveyed the impression that she understood Reiki. Or at least was respectful of it since I'd been there a few times and David was showing a slight uptick, at least in producing urine. It was something positive in spite of the dire news.

We went into his room. I looked down at the catheter bag and saw there was indeed more urine in it than there had been the day before. I was genuinely excited. I viewed it as a sign that he was really fighting hard to live, no matter how daunting the odds. I decided to focus on this one positive evidence of improvement. Nearing the bed, I greeted David with the good news.

"Hi David," I said cheerily. "It's Scarlett."

The heart monitor showed an increase in his heartbeats. I didn't know whether or not this was good, but since it leveled off, I figured it was his way of telling me he was glad I had returned.

"I'm here for your Reiki treatment today. It looks like you're doing a great job of healing! Did you hear that you produced more urine this morning? That means your kidneys are healing! Isn't that great?"

David's eyelids, though still firmly shut, fluttered a bit. "Do I have your permission to work with you today?"

I waited. I could feel his affirmative response like a little whoosh of breeze. I paused for a moment—because he was Jewish, I wanted to be respectful—aware that having said my prayers during the ride over and in the hospital parking lot had brought me to a place where I felt it appropriate to speak out loud some of the affirmative wisdom I had learned while serving on the prayer team at the Unity Christ Church that I formerly attended.

I believe in the healing power of Jesus. I had studied the biblical teachings on healing and attended a Pentecostal church with my mom when I was 16. While there, I was baptized in the Holy Spirit and felt that loving healing energy flow through me. My mom, a professional nurse, affirmed that I had been given the gift of healing. At the time, I did not know what I would do with this gift, but now it seemed to be working through me with David. The Reiki energy healing system uses the same universal force that Jesus demonstrated as a healing tool. It is, however, not related to any particular religion and therefore would not infringe on David's personal beliefs.

I told him, "I am praying for your protection and mine."

Being extra careful because he had the oxygen monitor on his index finger and needles taped to the back of his hand, I reached for his hand and carefully clasped it in both of mine. There was still no grip or other noticeable response. I took a deep breath and reminded myself mentally that I was there to channel love and healing.

"There is nothing but love for you here today. David, think about all the love that is surrounding you. Remember that everyone who loves you is praying for you right now. Even people you don't know, care about you. If you believe in guardian angels, then I'm asking yours to be here right now with us. Only the highest and best forces surround us. Only the most holy beings work with us today and always. The love enfolding you is healing love. Let's begin."

I began to synchronize my breathing with the ventilator. I could feel my heart rate change as I matched my breaths with his. I placed my other hand gently on his forehead, smoothing back his hair in a maternal way. The emotions of compassion and empathy overwhelmed me and I felt my eyes smart with tears. My entire body felt coiled and energized with a gut-level connection. My hands were tingling when I entered the room; now they were like hot irons. As I stood there, holding his hand and keeping my other hand on his forehead, I could feel a pulse beat throughout my being. My entire body was pulsing and my heartbeat felt like it was synced with his. Our breathing and heartbeats were now as if one. That's when my sense of consciousness switched and I was no longer in my body.

It seemed that I was in a swirl, like an energy vortex. Then, just as quickly as I had felt that I had been sucked through this energy pathway, I felt I was deposited on the other side of it. Here, everything was calm and quiet. The sound of machines and other noise had disappeared. There was nothing but light, like millions of points of it, all pulsing, all alive, all breathing. It resembled a luxurious fabric that I could walk through and breathe in, engulfing me in a bath of liquid love unlike anything I had experienced before.

This must be heaven, I thought. There was nothing but love, complete and total peace, and a sense of bliss that was impossible to describe. I experienced an enormous sense of wellbeing and joy. I was breathing the light and the light was breathing me. I was a part of the whole—in unity with the All. This experience of unconditional love was pure euphoria.

It took me some time to orient to this awareness of being in what had to be my etheric body. I knew I was out of my physical body. My spiritual eyes adjusted and appearing almost in parts, I could see my physical form. I could see that I was standing in this light amid the millions of droplets of love raining down, floating and sparkling as they fell.

Then I felt the presence of someone standing in the light next to me. At first, I could not see who it was. Yet, I sensed my hand was intertwined with another. It was the essence of David, light-filled and radiant; his being pulsating with the light. I was overjoyed to see him and he was jubilant to see me. We were talking telepathically—communing with our minds. I felt I had arrived home with my other half.

Now I understood why I felt it was such a privilege and honor to be with him. I knew what I owed him. I could sense information pouring in, filling my mind with an intelligence that was the purest form of knowledge transfer I'd ever experienced. My mind comprehended everything all at once; I *knew* the answers to all my spiritual questions. I *knew* that everything in my life was meant to be and that there had been no mistakes, just choices. I understood the paradox of destiny and free will—something that had always confused me. The timelessness of love and connection was revealed. And that we truly are eternal beings who have the incredible gift and opportunity to be incarnate in this world. I perceived that I chose to be here and that my path was to help people remember they were here to learn to love.

I *knew* David and I shared a sacred bond that transcended time. We have always been together. We are a part of each other; our cosmic DNA is entwined. His life energy and my life energy were enveloped together with a third force—the love-light energy breathing through us; threading through us like a triple helix.

I knew he had called me and had waited for me. I knew I had resisted going because I had given up and had lost my faith and hope, just as he had. I knew that "the love," which are the only words that makes sense to describe this force, had brought us together in spite of ourselves at the very last moment. *This is my mate from the forever time. Now, we have found each other and the joy is indescribable. I know we are connected with an unbreakable bond—beyond this life, beyond death. We have been together forever and will be together for eternity. As above, so below. On earth, as it is in heaven.* I could feel these truths permeating our etheric bodies.

David was showing me feelings from his present physical life and all that had happened on this journey. The emotions seemed to swirl, folding over and merging together with him watching the events while I internalized the feelings involved.

We were holding hands, at peace to be together in this timeless place. It's not so much that we were breathing but that we were being breathed by the light. I have never felt a love so great or experienced such a connectedness with another being. And the fruits of love, such as healing, forgiveness, compassion, kindness, and unconditional acceptance, were all that mattered. I knew that all the challenges in our lives had been footfalls on the path to grace. There was no question that this was a state of grace we were in.

Suddenly the light droplets began to disperse and grow thinner. Things were becoming dimmer and I was being pulled away. My essence began to fade. With a whoosh, I was back in the dimly lit hospital room, standing at David's side, still holding his hand. I noticed that he looked different. He seemed to be lighter and more radiant, but still unconscious.

Now here we were, plunked back to earth and the jolting reality of our humanness. To say I was rattled and confused would be an understatement. I felt I had entered into an arena of consciousness that I had never before encountered in quite that way. That was the paradox—my human self was acutely aware of his human self with all its frailties, bad choices and imperfections, and yet there was this huge love that embraced it all as part of the learning experiences of his life.

God works in mysterious ways, I thought. All I knew is there is a huge force far more powerful than me and that force was in charge of this whole thing. I knew I was meant to be there. I was grateful to be there and it was a privilege to share this time with him. It was the least I could do. None of this made sense rationally, but these were the emotions and the knowing that swept over me.

The love was still circling around us and the radiant energy was still pulsing as I glanced at the clock. Only a few minutes had passed while I was in that state of heightened awareness.

Next I began the Reiki treatment, listening for the intuitive guidance that would show me what needed to be done. My right hand was vibrating seemingly with the speed of a jackhammer while hovering over his kidney area. My left hand (the guider hand, I called it) was also vibrating, but steadier, almost like a lightning rod channeling the energy while my right hand was applying that energy. My hand continued to hover over his kidneys; the energy swirled as I began to talk.

"I'm working with your kidneys now. I'm going to talk directly to them, David. They are a part of you, but they have their own life force and I'm going to find out what they need."

It sounded crazy, but I knew it worked. I leaned forward and began talking to his kidneys. I thanked them for the incredible job they were doing and how wonderfully they were working. I affirmed that they were healthy and whole, fully functioning and filled with sacred light and loving energy. I could feel the energy shifting, as though the illness in the kidneys was being magnetized out of his body and pulling toward my vibrating hand. The speed of the vibration was somehow diffusing the illness. I told his kidneys that they had permission to release any and all negative energy. I affirmed that his kidneys no longer recognized this illness, thus the disease could not stay because the frequency had changed. My hand was still vibrating but the frequency, like a musical chord, was slowing its vibration. I continued telling his kidneys that they were completely healed and I thanked God for their full restoration.

Frank arrived for a visit just as I was finishing up the Reiki treatment. I gave him a hug and told him that things seemed to be going well.

As a result of our spiritual experience, my curiosity about David was really piqued. And since I hadn't seen Frank after our get-together the previous week because I had been so caught up in activities, I invited him to go with me for a cup of coffee and tell me a little about his friend. I squeezed David's hand and told him I would be back later.

As Frank and I headed for the hospital cafeteria, he began to fill me in on David's background. David had come to town to work as a contractor for a financial services firm in February because he had been laid off from his job on the West Coast and the job in Richmond was the only employment he could find. This job was originally to last for about a year, but he had been offered a permanent position just a few weeks before he got sick and entered the hospital.

Frank proceeded to tell me that David was either divorced or on his way to a divorce, as far as he knew.

I also asked him about David's mother. Frank told me that Dee and David's dad, Bruce, and brother, Stephen, had all flown to Richmond for this last visit.

"I didn't meet Bruce or Stephen," I said.

He explained that Dee and Bruce were divorced but were very close friends. He also said that Dee had a partner who had not been able to fly out.

"Partner?"

"Yeah. Her partner is a woman."

"Well, that increases her coolness factor," I laughed. I was even more intrigued with David. "Having a mom who is a lesbian is a very interesting dynamic, especially since that's the topic in my class this week."

"Lesbians are your topic?"

"Well, this week we're talking about alternative lifestyles, including lesbian, gay, bisexual, and transgendered. It might be interesting to talk about gay and lesbian parents and see what the class's experience has been with them."

Fatigue had started to settle in. I had carried on back in this reality as though everything was business as usual. Actually, I was still floating from the after-effects of the experience with David. Now, after talking with Frank, I was beginning to wonder if it had just been a waking dream or a sort of hypnotic trance, but quickly dismissed those thoughts, realizing that the loving feelings and effusive expansion in my spirit were continuing to pulse through my body.

I headed home. Crossing the bridge, I noted that the James River water looked amazingly calm. The air was crisp and slightly cool, but the sky was still sunny. The trees looked unusually beautiful—perhaps this was their final hurrah before fall changed their colors.

I was reflecting on how vibrantly alive and breathtaking everything seemed and then I was at my front door, not even remembering having driven the rest of the way. I fumbled with the door lock, stepped into the hall, dropped my purse and keys on the entryway table, and headed for the couch, where I fell into a deep sleep for about an hour until Ryan got home and woke me.

Chapter 9
Healing Helpers

Tuesday, September 27, 2005

As a graduate teaching assistant, I taught two back-to-back classes in Criminal Justice on Tuesdays and Thursdays. The second class ended shortly before noon. After it was over, I beelined to the hospital. As usual, I prayed during the drive over. Once I found a parking space in the jammed lot, I paused before getting out to pray in Jesus' name. It was lunchtime at St. Mary's and the place was crowded with cars coming and going. Excited to see how David was doing, I raced up the escalator and onto the elevator.

Then I rushed to the Cardiac Care Unit and rang the nurse's station for permission to enter. The nurse buzzed me in immediately. I entered David's room to find a woman jiggling a large machine that was hooked up to him. It was making loud popping noises, like a gun backfiring. The woman seemed frustrated and concerned. I glanced at David; he was still locked in unconsciousness. Puzzled about what was going on, I introduced myself.

"I'm Connie," she said. "I'm here to do a dialysis treatment on David, but I'm having trouble with the machine." Her large dangling earrings, each shaped in the letter *C*, swayed as she adjusted the tubes. She eyed me somewhat suspiciously.

"I'm here to pray with him." At the sound of my voice, David's heart monitor spiked, showing an increase in his heartbeat.

"He likes you, honey," she said. "Not like the other lady who was here just a while ago, saying she was praying for him, but all she did was mess up my machine," she harrumphed.

I couldn't imagine who had come to pray with him. The hospital chaplain was a man.

I said, "Well, let's see if we can get things calmed down. Connie, would you be willing to pray with me?"

"Yes."

I asked her to take David's hand and mine as I held his other hand for the three of us to form a prayer circle. She and I both bowed our heads and I began praying out loud, and thanked God for David's healing and affirmed our gratitude that God was using all sources in heaven and earth to surround him with love and wellbeing. I gave thanks for the successful dialysis treatment and the presence of caring people, like Connie, who were doing all they could to help him.

"Yes, Jesus," Connie joined in.

I continued my prayer as Connie harmonized, "Thank you, Lord. Thank you, Jesus."

I felt the bonds of love surrounding us all. Although I knew the need to respect David's belief in Judaism, I was grateful for Connie's presence and her unrestrained "thank you" to Jesus. As I concluded the prayer, the dialysis machine also seemed to calm down. There was less hissing and popping now.

Connie and I let go of each other's hands but when our eyes met, I could tell she was also a powerful spiritual healer who used the machines as her healing ministry. God uses us all, it seems, each in accordance with our unique calling.

As the dialysis continued, I explained to her, "I'm going to do some laying on of hands healing."

"I understand. They do that at my church."

I asked her to keep the prayers going while I began Reiki with David. Today was different—I felt no need to speak aloud to him. I could now telepathically connect with his mind and feel his happiness over my presence with him. I paused to look at his face. Some of the swelling had gone down and he looked more human. He still had all the tubes in his mouth and his nose, but somehow he seemed more present. I felt a rush of affection for him in that moment. I reached over and gently, motherly, smoothed his hair back from his brow.

I began feeling his energy levels with my hands; soon they were hot and tingling. The energy was swirling; he was absorbing and recirculating it, almost the way the dialysis machine was filtering his blood and returning it to his body.

Connie and I worked in companionable silence. As I moved around the bed, she shifted slightly, wheeling the machine off to the side as I circled the bed for the final wrap-up.

Just then, Joe entered the room. I had met Joe briefly years ago at a church I used to attend. I wasn't sure why he had come or what the connection could be, so I asked him.

"I work for the Social Security Administration," he explained. "I'm going to leave paperwork for David so he can file for disability if he pulls through. I was told that if he lives, he will be permanently disabled. If he regains consciousness, I'll come back to help him or his family members fill out the forms." I was surprised that he was saying this as though David couldn't hear him. I knew David could and I gave his hand a little squeeze of reassurance.

We talked a bit, rather loudly. I was concerned that we were disturbing David because I could feel a shift in the room's energy, moving from a focus on David to the interaction between Joe, Connie, and me. Then another nurse came in to check on things. We all were chatting around David's bed, rejoicing over the fact that he was now showing more urine than he had before in his catheter bag. It was hard to believe we could get excited by this but we eagerly claimed every hopeful sign as a positive indication of recovery. Joe then made a noisy departure, and Connie began disconnecting the dialysis machine as the treatment had concluded.

I gave Connie a hug. "Thank you for being here."

When everyone left, I refocused on connecting with David.

"I will be back to see you tomorrow. And remember, I am only a thought away—and not even that far." I wasn't sure why I used those words, but it felt like we were connected in such an instantaneous way that a thought away seemed too far.

I leaned over and kissed his forehead, like I used to kiss my children when they were sick. I gave his hand a gentle squeeze. "Hang in there, David. You're doing great and you're making an incredible comeback."

My words were more confident sounding than I actually felt, but the power of words must not be underestimated.

I left the room, feeling lighter, almost festive.

When I stepped outside, the afternoon sun was still shining, but the air was starting to cool down, with a hint of crispy fall coolness making me shiver. Fall was going to be especially beautiful this year; I could tell by the early turning of the leaves. David had gone into the hospital at the end of summer and now Fall was beginning. The seasons were making a gradual shift, just like David.

CHAPTER 10

LIFE LESSONS: WHO IS IT OKAY TO HATE?

Wednesday, September 28, 2005

As I'd told Frank, the class today was about alternative lifestyles. I had a diverse mix of students from many countries with a variety of beliefs. In addition, one male student was openly gay.

During a previous class, a small cadre of conservative religious students had expressed disapproval of homosexuality. I had suggested we table the discussion until we reached that particular chapter in the assigned text. That way, everyone could read the chapter and be prepared for a more informed discussion.

We opened with a discussion about sexuality being fluid. John, the openly gay student, talked about male inmates who had sex with men while in prison but did not consider themselves to be gay. He explained it was sex with the only gender available to these inmates and generally they went back to heterosexual relationships upon release from prison.

I had hoped the students would be open-minded based on the theories of different strokes for different folks and live and let live. However, I was wrong. The class discussion immediately became contentious.

John said, "I am tired of being judged for being gay." He then told the story of a recent hate crime committed against a woman because she was a lesbian.

The group of conservative students had a main ringleader, Devon, who was loudly vocal in his opinions.

"Well, the Bible says it's a sin and you're going to hell!" Devon declared emphatically. He was joined by a chorus of "that's right" from the small flock of young women who sat with him in each class.

"Well, intolerant people can go to hell too!" John snapped in his own defense.

In addition to the lifestyle issue, there was an undercurrent of racial tension. John was short and white. Devon was tall and black. I could see that things were quickly going to spin out of control and could even become violent. Shouting began to erupt as Devon started to rise from his seat, struggling to unfold his body from the desk/chair combo.

"Whoa class!" I yelled to be heard over the arguing students. "Devon, sit down!"

Devon looked at me, defiance on his face. He sat down resentfully. "It's a sin," he repeated. "It says so in the Bible."

"The Bible says that slaves should obey their masters. Do you agree with that?" I asked.

Devon stared at me, sullen and sour.

"There are many things in the Bible that are open to interpretation. But the Bible also teaches love and acceptance. Devon, have you ever been judged for the color of your skin?"

Still defiant, Devon stared at me. He grudgingly nodded. "Well, that's not the same thing. I was born this way. I didn't choose to be black."

"I want you all to think about this and think hard." I paused to let my words sink in. "How does it feel to have someone judge you based on your skin color? Not very good, does it? How does it feel to have someone who doesn't even know you decide at first glance they hate you because of the color of your skin? Not good, right? You're a human being with people in your life who love you. And you, by your humanity, are worthy, just as you stand. You can't help being born black any more than John can help being born gay. It's in his genetic code."

"I think it's a choice," Devon said.

"Yeah, right," John snapped. "Do you think a gay person chooses to be gay? Do you think I woke up one day and decided I wanted to be gay and have to either hide who I am or have people like *you* hate me and make my life a living hell or beat the shit out of me? Do you think I would choose this?"

The class grew quiet. John was quivering, his eyes filled with tears. The pain in his voice tugged at my heart. I knew this was a teachable moment.

I addressed the class. "Does it seem to you that those who are gay are treated by some people the same way that black people historically were? Blacks were beaten, lynched, and killed just for being black. Gays are being beaten, raped, and killed just for being gay. What do you think about that?"

I paused, looking first at Devon, then at John. "I'm wondering if you have more in common than you think."

My mantra to the students was: *Think about it! Just think about it!* As an instructor, I felt the most meaningful contribution I could make was to guide my students to seriously contemplate life and its complexities. That way, they could develop informed values as they prepared to take their places in the world.

Another one of my mantras was *Be conscious out there!* Many of the class concepts were challenging to conventional thinking and our discussions held the potential to raise consciousness.

The next words to roll spontaneously from my mouth surprised me. It turned out to be one of the best classes in my teaching career. "Who is it okay to hate?"

The class was quiet now, reflecting. No one responded.

"People tend to hate those who are different from them. They hate them if their skin color is different, their sexual orientation is different, or their religion is different. Look at all the wars being fought over religion—each one believing it is the only right one. So, if you believe that *your* religion is the only right one, everyone else, by default, has to be wrong. If they're wrong, they're different. People tend to hate what's different. And when they hate those who are different, they want to kill them.

"Remember what happened to Jesus in the Bible? Think about the Holocaust. Hitler convinced the Germans that the Jews, the disabled, the homosexuals and any others who weren't part of his idea of a superior race should be rounded up like cattle and killed. The sad part is that he convinced a multitude of people to believe him. He whipped them into a hate-filled frenzy. Then because they felt superior, because they believed they were the only people who were worthwhile, every other human being's humanity was dismissed. Those different ones were viewed as *contemptible others* worth nothing; to be used, humiliated, tortured, and killed. That's what hate does. It destroys one's sense of humanity."

The room had the attentive hushed silence that happens in certain moments when you know you have totally engaged a group.

"Hate kills, doesn't it? I am looking around this room right now and see a mix of students who could be Christian, Jewish, Hindu, atheist, agnostic, or whatever religion, who may be gay, straight, black, white, brown, yellow. And who are male, female, and maybe transgender. Every one of you has, at some point, experienced prejudice and unwarranted hate just for being who you are, for being who you were born to be.

"I want you to take a moment, look around at each other and see what I see. I see a group of human beings who are very different, but still human. I see you all as smart, capable, and worthwhile people who want what most humans desire: love and acceptance.

"This is a class about relationships. However tonight, this is a class about understanding that we have one major shared relationship. We share a connection and a relationship with each other as human beings. We are united—in our differences—by our humanity.

"So look around the room. Perceive each other as human beings who are more than skin, bone, and beliefs. And if you can, see yourselves as one human family."

I paused, letting the words sink in. Class was almost over. It had been an intense experience for us all.

I noticed that the students were looking around. John and Devon even made eye contact, albeit brief and furtive. *Progress!* I thought.

"Now, tell me: Who is it ok to hate?"

I turned away to head back to the lectern.

"Your assignment this week is to write one page about an experience you may have personally had or witnessed about someone being scorned for no reason other than their race, gender, sexual orientation, religion, ethnicity, or national origin. See you next class."

I hastily packed my folder and notes, ready to head to the hospital. The class quickly cleared, except for John. He appeared tense as he stood watching me, shifting from foot to foot. I wasn't sure what he wanted to say, but it was clear something was on his mind.

"Um, thank you for what you said today."

"You're welcome. I hope it helped open some minds."

His answer surprised me. "It helped me to open mine, too. See you later."

John scurried out. I paused for a moment, feeling the void of the empty classroom.

I had sat in these rooms off and on for more than two decades, struggling along as a student. Now here I was standing at the lectern, facing the students sitting in the same chairs I had used year after year. Thoughts raced through my mind.

It was such an honor and responsibility to teach. Human beings are so fragile and everyone just stumbles down paths, trying to live their lives the best way they can. I hoped that my students left the class today with a changed perspective. On the other hand, I knew that people will truly hear only what they want or need.

The class had changed me, too, and reminded me of something important: opening hearts and minds would always be my passion. My class was teaching me to follow my heart. I was grateful to John for having the courage to be who he is; I felt compassion for him in his suffering just to be an authentic human being. "Will we ever transcend our differences?" I wondered.

I sighed and headed out to the parking deck. It was a 15-minute drive to the hospital and I was eager to see David.

When I got to the hospital and phoned in, the nurse told me I would need to wait for a while. They were giving David a bath. I sat patiently in the waiting room, surprised by the sense of calm that swept over me. I was transported to a place of peace with feelings of love and gratitude gently filling my being. Ordinarily, I would have fidgeted impatiently, stewing that I was wasting time. But not today. I knew in my heart I was doing God's work, and everything was just as it should be. I closed my eyes and prayed. About 45 minutes passed before the nurse greeted me. "David opened his eyes a bit today and was able to move his arms. In fact, he tried to pull his feeding tube out! He's been feisty today." She laughed.

This was great news. But when I went in, his eyes were closed. I was disappointed, having hoped his eyes might be open. I didn't even know what color they were.

"Hey David, it's me, Scarlett. I hear you've been feisty today! Giving the nurses a hard time, are you? Well, that's great. You're on your way to a great recovery. Are you ready to get to work today?"

I waited for the gentle waft of breeze, but that didn't come. The energy in the room felt different. David's swelling seemed to have gone down and there were splotches of color in his cheeks. The machines were still beeping and the respirator was still making its rhythmic rasp. Extra tape held the feeding tube in place—I could see it would make it harder for him to yank out, but not impossible if he gave it a good tug: I doubted he had that much strength anyway, given how nonresponsive he was now. Soon, however, the energy began to crackle and David's heart monitor spiked.

"Happy to see me, huh?" I teased. "Well, let's get started. I'm going to take your hand and we'll begin with our prayer of gratitude for all the great healing that's taking place. Sound good?"

I reached for his hand, just as I had done in all the previous visits. As my hand gently clasped his, I was amazed to feel his fingers clasp around mine—his finger monitor became slightly dislodged from the movement. I was thrilled at the first sign of physical responsiveness. He was holding on with a noticeable grip. I began my opening prayer.

"Dear God, David and I give thanks today for your miraculous healing presence. We know that all things come from you and we are grateful for this sacred healing time. I give thanks to you, to all the forces in your universe that are sacred and holy, and I know that only the highest and best outcome will be granted today. Thank you, God."

I finished the prayer and stood quietly, feeling the loving communion between us. David gently squeezed my hand. That gentle squeeze inexplicably touched me. All of a sudden, I was overcome with emotion and began to cry tears of happiness and joy. Then David's heart monitor began to spike.

"It's okay. I'm crying because I'm happy to feel your hand move," I said softly.

I could feel him calm down. The tightness in my chest that always comes when I cry slowly eased. I began to breathe deeply and to synchronize my breathing with David and the respirator. When our breathing was in unison, I felt the energy of our connection begin to whirl as it emerged uncontrollably from my quivering body, almost quaking from head to toe. David's body was radiating and absorbing the loving energy that spilled out of me while I focused on my breathing, relaxing into it.

"We're working on your lungs today," I told David. "We've got to get your lungs breathing on their own. Your lungs are healthy, vibrant and full of light and energy. They are completely healed and restored. Your lungs, David, are powerful and strong. They are healthy and filled with the loving, healing air of God's breath. Every breath you take is breathing in God's healing energy. Every breath out is releasing anything that is not of God. Breathe in God, David, breathe in the love."

I stood still, breathing with him. My hands were moving fast over his lung area. My left hand cupped in the air over his lung area, and my right hand moved back and forth like I was erasing something. My hand was moving so fast that it blurred as I looked at it. I couldn't believe the precision and the speed. All of a sudden, I could feel the energy stop. It was done and I was finished for the day.

It seemed to be an abrupt cut-off, but I was used to the energy doing what it needed to do. I was merely the vessel through which it passed. David's eyelids were fluttering. For a brief moment, he barely opened his eyes and stared ahead. Then, he closed them and faded back into unconsciousness.

"Thank you, David, for your hard work today in accepting and using the energy. I will be back tomorrow. Meanwhile, the energy will continue to work within your body, so simply allow it do its work."

I leaned over and gently kissed his forehead. He squeezed my hand again. I left, all at once overcome with weariness. I needed a nap. An enormous amount of energy had flowed through me—I was both abuzz and drained from it.

By the time I got home I no longer desired a nap. Ryan and James would be home soon and would need help with homework. I also wanted to figure out what to make for dinner. Ryan was picky and moody these days. I was trying hard to keep a healthy diet, but he, like most kids, wanted junk. James would eat most anything. I knew both boys would eat chicken, so I cut on the oven to preheat and figured I'd cook some chicken in barbeque sauce and serve it with rice and broccoli. Ryan generally ate that without too much fuss. After dinner, Tim would pick up James and head over to their house for the night. So far, co-parenting was working out for us all. It wasn't ideal but it was the best solution and I was grateful we were doing okay with it.

Next, I called my healing friends, Cherie and Doug, and shared with Cherie my mixture of feelings. The two had recently married after many years of living together. Both were Reiki masters and teachers and I felt I needed help in unblocking some of the strong emotions that urged me onward toward what appeared to be an unknown destination. I was experiencing a more intense yearning for a loving partner in my life.

I had talked to Greg the night before to let him know what was happening with David. Since he didn't seem interested in asking me out, I let it go. But I was disappointed and confused, wondering why my yearning was stronger than ever while Greg was acting more distant.

Assuming I must have some blocked energy, I thought Cherie and Doug could help me clear the blockage. Also, my vital energy felt a bit drained. Perhaps it would help to have a healing session with them and be recharged. Cherie told me to come the next day. I knew I could talk to them both and they would offer good insights.

Chapter 11
Miracle Boy

Thursday, September 29, 2005

In addition to my course on Relationships, I served as a Graduate Teaching Assistant for a beginning level Criminal Justice class.

I had a more advanced criminal justice class immediately after the first one, so I had to scurry across campus to make it to the second one—there was only a ten-minute window between the two classes, which made it nearly impossible to make it to the next session on time, especially if I had to take a bathroom break.

I made it through my double-duty classes, sprinted to the parking deck, and drove to the hospital to visit David.

Today, I felt energized and was excited to see how David was doing, especially after yesterday's powerful healing session. Nurse Sherrie buzzed me in. She was waiting for me at the door. I felt immediately alarmed as though something was wrong. Then she burst into a big smile.

"Come see *Miracle Boy*. That's what we're calling him now."

Not knowing what to expect, I rushed past her into his room. The respirator tube was out and he was breathing on his own. His breath was very ragged and there were some long pauses between breaths, but he was doing it.

And he was awake, his eyes wide open like a child's. I was surprised to see he had dark brown eyes—the same color as mine. Although he looked at me with a fixed stare, he displayed no sign of recognition; however, I wasn't expecting him to know me, and besides he was still heavily medicated.

"Hi David—it's so good to see you awake." I was excited.

I turned to the nurse and asked, "When did this happen?"

"He woke up this morning around 11. We noticed he didn't need the respirator this morning, so we took the tube out. As you can see, he's having a rough time and we don't know if it will stay out, but this is a huge improvement."

"Wow, to say the least."

"I know. That's why we're calling him *Miracle Boy*," she smiled. "I don't know exactly what you're doing, but whatever it is, keep it up. I'll let you get to work."

She left and I turned to David. This was the first time I'd seen him awake. Our eyes met and he lifted his hand out to me. His arm was shaking with the strain of it, so I quickly reached over to clasp his hand.

"Welcome back." I smiled at him and stared into his eyes. It felt like we had known each other forever but were now meeting for the first time. His breath was coming out in little rasps. His lips were swollen, cracked and dry. I made a mental note to ask the nurse for some lip balm when she returned.

"We're going to work some more on your lungs today. I know you don't want that breathing tube back, right?"

David continued to look at me, his face expressionless. It didn't matter. As far as I was concerned, this was a true miracle. I knew he wasn't out of the woods yet, so we were going to continue with our prayers of gratitude and healing.

I realized that I was more uncertain than before of what to expect from the energy flow, but I was willing to trust

God and go along with it. I used the same procedure as the day before. As the energy began to swirl between us, I could sense a different connection beginning to occur. This felt as though we were making a conscious connection in addition to the established spiritual one. It shifted the energy a bit and now I felt a little self-conscious. What must he think about me and about all this? He didn't know me at all, so he was basically waking up to see a strange woman smiling at him, holding his hand and saying prayers over him as though they were long-lost friends. But as the energy built, my self-consciousness dissipated.

I had closed my eyes to pray. When I opened them, David's were closed. He was gripping my hand now with new strength. The energy flowed and we focused on his lungs. David's breathing eased and he seemed to go into a light sleep. I continued my healing prattle, my voice soft and soothing, then was overwhelmed with gratitude at the miracle that was taking place before my eyes. I knew I was sharing in something that was bigger and more amazing than anything I had ever before encountered. I was astonished, moved, and humbled, all at once. The energy still made my whole body vibrate, but it wasn't as jarring as it had been yesterday. It felt more controlled. And, just as before, when it was done, it was done, and that was it.

I thanked David for the opportunity to share this sacred time with him. I assured him that I was committed and would continue to see him through this, if that's what he also chose.

Just then, the nurse quietly knocked on the door. I had noticed that most of the nursing staff were treating me more respectfully now. They acknowledged that my work with David deserved quiet and uninterrupted time.

"David's lips are looking pretty dry and cracked. Do you have any lip balm or something that might help?" I asked her.

"I'll get some," she said and left the room. I held David's hand a bit longer, and he gently squeezed mine. The nurse came back with a small tube of lip gel and a few cotton swabs.

"Here. Do you want to do it?"

I nodded and she handed the tube to me along with one of the swabs. I squeezed a small amount onto the tip and gently applied it to his lips until a strand of the cotton swab unraveled and stuck to his lip. I tried to move it off with the swab, but it was mired in the gel. A moment later I carefully plucked it off.

"Okay. That should moisten your lips for a while. Remember, you're doing great. And that breathing tube is going to stay out. I'll see you tomorrow." I gave his forehead a kiss; he gave my hand a slight squeeze.

When I arrived at Cherie and Doug's farmhouse, a flood of relief swept over me. Spending time with them would soothe my soul. Cherie had horses, dogs, cats, and lots of land for the animals to roam. I always felt better while in the country, surrounded by nature.

Doug wasn't home yet, so Cherie and I had time to chat. As I walked into their kitchen, I saw her prayer list posted on the wall. I was stunned to see David's name on the list. I had not talked to Cherie or Doug about the recent events, so I couldn't imagine how they had gotten his name.

"Cherie! David is the man in the hospital who I've been doing Reiki with. How do you know him?"

"I don't know him," Cherie explained. "But Sheila does. She told us about him and asked that we pray for him. She said he was a friend of hers who became suddenly ill and now was dying."

"I didn't know that you knew Sheila. This is getting strange."

Cherie continued, "Sheila is one of my former Reiki students. She took her first and second level trainings with me."

"What a small world, but that's to be expected with us, isn't it?" I said.

I related all that had been going on with Greg, David, and my own life.

"I'm concerned that I have some emotional stumbling blocks preventing me from being with my soul mate. Plus, I feel that my effectiveness as a healing channel could be improved if these blocks were removed. It would be good for me to have my energy field cleared."

Soon afterwards, Doug came home and we caught up on everything. Minutes later I was on the massage table. With the soft lights, gentle music, and two sets of healing hands, I was transported. Suddenly, I sensed the energy of my father coming through Doug—but my father had often been scary to me. Doug must have sensed that, and his energy now transmuted my father's presence into a loving and gentle form. I could feel those old wounds and blocks dissolve. The issues with my dad that had affected my relationships seemed to be smoothed over like a wooden ridge well sandpapered.

The pain flew away like dust particles and all that remained was a gleaming spirit. Doug's fatherly energy was safe and soothing as I felt a paternal love I'd always yearned for surround me. The fear of being hurt was gone. I felt safe, loved, and cared for—something I had never before experienced with men.

Tears of release trickled from my eyes. Doug gently wiped my tears and then held my hand, just as I usually held David's. I could feel Doug's love flowing into me. Cherie was at my feet, harmoniously sending her loving maternal energy. Bathed in a loving parental energy that balanced male and female, a new sense of strength awakened within my spirit. I was healed and whole and changed at a core level.

Profoundly grateful to them both, I promised to share this extra energy boost with David. In essence, their healing energy would be flowing through me, in addition to my own. I looked forward to seeing David the next day, already wondering whether this combined healing energy would indeed be stronger.

CHAPTER 12
COMMITMENT

Friday, September 30, 2005

My Marriage and Family class was subdued today. We were discussing the true meaning of our marriage vows and how most people mouth the words without any real understanding. Then we talked about the characteristics of commitment.

"So think about it. To what are we committing when we vow to love someone *'For richer or poorer, for better or worse, in sickness and in health, until death do us part?'*

"What is the number one reason couples get divorced?"

"Money!" several students yelled out.

"That's just about right—it's *fights* over money issues that are one of the biggest reasons for divorce. But health issues are also a big deal-breaker for many. What happens when your partner isn't doing well and maybe is in a lifelong depression? What happens if they develop an addiction or had one to begin with—how would you handle drugs, alcohol, porn, gambling, food, and any other potential health calamities in a relationship? What happens if you manage to make it through those landmines only to have a baby born with a major disability?"

I paused to let that sink in.

"That seems to blow many marriages and relationships apart. And then what happens when one partner gets really sick or becomes disabled? Would you love them then?

"I'm not trying to be depressing, but this is a class about love and commitment. You need to know what that really means—that life will be life and marriage is hard. That's why the divorce rate is so high. Commitment is hard. But love—real love—can make it through all those challenges. This class is about exploring marriage and family relationships that work or don't work and understanding why in either case."

Then we talked about the exchange theory of relationships, which is basically a set of trades. For example, a man may want an attractive woman while the woman may desire a man who makes a good salary. They decide to exchange those attributes and call it a relationship. It's really nothing more than a trade-off. And that, unfortunately, is the basis for too many relationships. "Is it any wonder the divorce rate is astronomical?"

I wanted to end the class on a positive note.

"Love is stronger than all possible adversities only when it is based on something more than fleeting attraction or trading demands. Can you think of any relationships among the people you know that demonstrate the kind you would like to have for yourself? Maybe something based on unconditional love? Is that a familiar term?"

The students shook their heads from side to side—their version of a collective *No.*

"Well, don't be discouraged. Next time we're going to discuss unconditional love."

As I drove to the hospital after class, I pondered David's life, wondering what had happened to him.

I must have been deep in thought, because I was parking my car in the hospital lot before I realized I had arrived.

The previous fifteen minutes had flown by in a trance. It seemed automatic now to drive to the hospital and head for the escalator. But with each visit I still felt nervous, not sure what I would find with David's health or what results the nurses would report.

I didn't like feeling attached to the outcome, but I was. It was not a comfortable experience for me because it interfered with my usual sense of detachment in place during a healing encounter. I had to admit that this was beyond anything I had ever done before, with his critical level of illness and the proportional exchange of energy that was taking place between David and me. When I got to the double doors and pressed the buzzer, Nurse Anne greeted me at the door. She had a concerned look on her face and was clearly blocking me from coming in. I was immediately alarmed.

"Has something happened?" I asked with a nervous edge to my voice.

Nurse Anne could see the alarm in my face and was quick to say, "No, no. He's actually doing better today. So much better that we need to clean him up. It might take a while, so if you'll kindly wait in the family area, we'll buzz you when he's ready to be seen."

Relief flooded through me. So that was it! He was doing better, which meant his other bodily functions were unexpectedly working! Which meant he needed a sponge bath! Good news indeed, even if it sounds messy. I headed for the family waiting area, surprised to feel calm and peaceful instead of impatient. All of my senses felt heightened; I was filled with a sense of joy and gratitude for this chance to be of service.

I decided to spend some time during my wait reflecting on why I felt a sense of responsibility for David, and why I felt so much gratitude that I could do something for him—the latter being influenced by my feelings that I owed him a portion of my healing services even though I was glad to serve. I did not know why and did not know if I ever would. Regardless of the reasons, I had to accept that there was a swirling within me of mixed feelings combined with a sense of time and place being multidimensional.

Rationally it didn't add up, but my spirit seemed to accept it all without a hitch, leaving me to feel like I was being split between two worlds.

Although I managed to regain my peacefulness, I was still eager to see David. I closed my eyes, trying to tune out the chatter of the other people in the waiting room and the low rumble of the television in the background. About 30 minutes later, Nurse Anne came to the door and motioned for me to come.

"He's awake," she said, smiling cheerfully at me. "Although being awake is a great improvement, he is not yet talking. We were able to take the feeding tube out. Well, actually, he pulled it out again. So we decided to see if he can swallow some liquids today. The nutritionist will be coming soon. We never know exactly when she'll be here, so it may interrupt your visit. I'm sorry about that, but just wanted to let you know."

"That's great news. We'll work on his throat then today," I answered.

I entered the room. There seemed to be less equipment. David's nose and mouth were free of tubes. I could see his face for the first time. His nose was slightly bent to the left from the presence of the ventilator tube having been in for nearly a month. His eyes were wide open and he seemed to be looking around the room as though he had never seen it before.

I quickly walked to his bed prepared to say a cheery hello. In that same instant he had turned his wide-eyed stare in my direction. His eyes, so huge and brown, locked with mine. The words I was about to say froze on my lips.

The all-encompassing love shining in his eyes took my breath away. There was a strange feeling now, a soul-deep sense of recognition and connection that rattled me to the bone. I could feel myself almost physically floating from the force of the love and the deep shared sense of connection. In a flash, I knew this man, I knew his soul, and I knew I loved him beyond anything I'd ever known. He knew me, too. I took a deep breath, and blinked, certain I had been seeing things.

The moment was broken as my rational mind kicked in. "This can't be," I told myself. "We just had a huge healing encounter and that's all this is."

I shook my head like I was shaking off beads of water.

"Hi David," I said, trying to make my voice sound extra cheerful. "I hear you're making great progress today and that things are functioning better than expected."

I laughed, trying to make a little joke. His eyes stayed locked on mine, unwavering in their expression of love and connection. I sighed, feeling squirmy now. I didn't know how to handle the overwhelming feelings that were making my stomach jump. The intense look in his eyes had not faded. He didn't speak—he couldn't as his throat was still swollen from the feeding tube.

"Well, shall we work on your throat today? It looks like you're going to be having a full course meal in no time!" I forced extra cheer in my voice, and hated the little quaver that seemed to betray me.

He nodded, still looking at me intently, then reached for my hand, his grip strong. I was unnerved. He didn't smile or change his expression.

I decided to resume our established routine. I gently squeezed his hand back, and moved my other hand to his third eye. He took a deep breath and closed his eyes, his head sinking into the pillow. I began the prayer, feeling a little self-conscious now, knowing he was awake and could hear me. Even though I knew he could hear me while unconscious, this was different.

I said the usual opening prayer and then placed my hand over his throat. The healing energy zoomed in again and it was now flowing from him into me and then back into him like a human dialysis machine as I continued my affirmative prayer.

"We give thanks for the soothing flow of energy that is now healing your throat. We give thanks that your throat and your body are ready to receive nourishment today. We give thanks for your continued healing. David, God is blessing you with love and healing today. Each day, you are getting stronger and better. I am so grateful for your amazing recovery and I thank God for the continued blessings and grace that God's love has given you."

I gently used my fingers to tap on his throat, like little raindrops sprinkling down. Very softly and very gently, the energy seemed to move from my fingers through the soft but purposeful tapping motion I made. Although the energy was as strong as it had always been, it seemed different, as though it was raining energy rather than pulsing it.

We were interrupted by the squeak of the hospital door opening. Nurse Anne came in, followed by a young woman pushing a cart. "Sorry to interrupt, but Nutrition is here."

I smiled at the woman and said, "Oh, that's perfect. It seems fitting I should be here when he takes his first sip of water. I can continue my work while you give it to him."

Nurse Anne and Lisa, the woman from Nutrition, rolled the cart over. She opened a little carton of applesauce, but changed her mind and opened some water, which she put on a small spoon. "Let's see if you can sip this first."

Carefully, she brought the spoon to his lips. My hand was on the back of his neck, the healing energy pulsing now. My other hand continued holding his. Like a baby bird, he opened his mouth and took a small sip from the spoon. The water seemed to go down without incident. She gave him another small sip and he swallowed that, too. Then he sputtered a little, coughing weakly.

"Well, that's a good start," Lisa said. Glancing at Nurse Anne, she said, "We'll come tomorrow to take him to X-ray to make sure the water went to the right place. If so, then we'll try the applesauce." She then looked at David. "You did a good job today! We'll go for the four-course meal tomorrow," she laughed.

David laid back and closed his eyes. The effort to swallow had taken a lot out of him. But he had done it and I had been there to witness his first sips.

After they left, I continued working on his throat chakra. As usual, the energy had a life all its own and I merely followed along, taking the spiritual guidance as if it was dictated. My hand paused over his throat, and then seemed to shake back and forth, small movements with amazing speed that continued for about one minute. I watched my hand moving so fast that it was blurry. Then it stopped and my hand hovered. I placed it gently on his throat and began my closing prayer. I knew we were done for the day. David had fallen into a deep sleep by now, his breath coming out in regular rhythms, but with a slight rasp. I thanked God for this amazing experience. I gently touched his forehead, gave his hand a small squeeze and headed out. I was elated and confused all at the same time.

As I drove away, I was grateful it was Friday. I would have some time to catch my breath this weekend and maybe reflect on all that had happened in such a short time. This was an amazing recovery, completely unexpected, and truly miraculous. But there was still so much unknown. For instance, David wasn't speaking. Would he ever be able to? I had gotten there in time and the healing work seemed to have stopped the brain stem from shutting down. However, there could be brain damage, nonetheless, that might reveal itself in the coming days.

Plus, David's kidneys, while beginning to function, were still not fully doing their job. He was scheduled for another dialysis treatment in the next few days. Clearly, there was more work to be done. I needed to rest and recharge if I was going to continue to be of service to him.

However, if I thought we'd already experienced some major transcendent experiences, I wasn't prepared for the next steps in the healing journey. The coming ones would stretch my understanding of spirituality, and the concept of other dimensions existing to help us, to an even greater awareness. David's healing journey was about to push me to a whole new level of understanding—one for which I wasn't sure I was ready.

But I seemed to not have a choice anymore. I had made a promise to David and I was going to see it through. I could sense that God wouldn't let me do otherwise.

Chapter 13
Healing Helpers from
Another Realm

Saturday, October 1, 2005

I woke up refreshed after a night of deep sleep, though I had awakened at some point in the night to feel David's presence in my room, his eyes looking at me as if to maintain our connection. I felt comforted that he was visiting and went back to sleep, snuggling into my pillow.

The morning was crisp and chilly. I felt really good and was looking forward to a quiet start, reading the paper and sipping coffee, and then later running some errands.

Ryan and I planned to go shopping for new sneakers. He had worn a hole in his most recent pair. Since he is rough on shoes, we planned to find a two-for-one special at the mall, hoping that having two pairs with which to alternate would mean both pairs would last longer. It was quiet at the mall except briefly when Ryan had a small meltdown after I said no to the pair of sneakers costing $125.

"Let's keep it in the $50 range," adding that $125 was a big expense for shoes that he would soon outgrow. Money was very tight and the ends seemed always to be ends.

After his whining did not work, he lashed out, "Forget about it. I'll wear the falling apart ones for gym class. I'll tell my teacher you are mean and won't buy me new sneakers."

Finally, we settled on a two-for-one special for $75. My son was happy and we would make do financially for the rest of the week.

Ryan planned to have a sleepover that night with his friend William. William's mom and I had discussed it and I had agreed to drive him to their house around five. She would bring him home the next morning.

Meanwhile, Greg had been out of town for the past week, but had been emailing me and some of our friends about David's progress. I wasn't sure what I would do tonight. My friend Jackie had an exciting date, so getting together with her was not an option. Thinking it would be nice to have an evening to myself, I decided to go see David and then on the way home stop by Blockbuster and rent a movie.

But when I got to the hospital, I was surprised and concerned to see that David's feeding tube had been reinserted. "What happened?" I asked Nurse Sherrie.

"It turned out that David got some of the water he drank yesterday into his lungs. It went down the wrong pipe, right David?"

"Is he okay?" I asked, worried that this was a terrible setback.

"It happens sometimes. We'll use the feeding tube for the next day or so and then try again with solids. That is, if David will let it stay in. He's been trying to pull it out again, haven't you, David?" She eyed him somewhat sternly.

I felt the quirk of a smile tug at my lips. He was really fighting back now.

"Well, we'll work on his throat and lungs today," I said, smiling at Nurse Sherrie and David. I tilted my head toward the door so she could see I wanted to step outside. She nodded her head in understanding and gave a small smile as we left the room.

"Is he really okay?" I asked.

"Yes, don't worry. This is not a big deal compared to everything else. We'll try again in another day or so." She smiled at me and headed to the nurse's station.

When I went back into David's room, he raised his shaky arms toward me, clearly wanting a hug. "Aw," I said, touched. I gave him an awkward hug and then took his hand. Although David's eyes were open, the look of recognition and deep connection with me was absent. Just a strong sense of affection. And I could see he had a little more clarity. His energy seemed to be flowing without much interference today.

"Sorry about the feeding tube going back in. We'll work on that. Next time, you'll be fine. You're still doing great, so don't worry about a little snag, okay?"

He nodded slightly. This was good. He understood what was being said, plus his eyes seemed to be tracking things better today.

"Let's start with our prayer." Holding his hand, just as I always did, I started the alignment with his third eye by placing my index finger over the area between his brows. I could feel the energy begin to hum.

Each visit seemed to elicit a different energy pattern and I was surprised to find how many variations of the energy there could be with one person. His overall energy pattern seemed to be stronger. However, there were definite differences in each area of his body, depending on the need for healing.

Today, his throat and lungs felt especially tingly, so that's where I focused my work. As I completed that part of the healing, I did the full body scan to wrap up. I could feel the energy over his kidney areas increase, feeling denser and more like sharp sparks pinging off my hand. This did not feel good to me and I was somewhat alarmed. Though I knew he was going to have another dialysis treatment in the next day or so, I figured we really needed to work on getting his kidneys functioning again.

David fell asleep in the middle of the treatment. I told him that I would work on him more tonight from home. I still don't know what made me say it, but I gently touched his third eye and said to him, "If you need me, remember, I'm only a thought away. Not even that far." I had said that to him before and it still felt true.

In that moment I was reminded of an experiment with quarks in physics. One quark could experience something and its twin quark, separated by thousands of miles, would instantaneously also experience it. The two, while separate and separated, were connected by an invisible force that united them as though they were one unit. That's how it felt with David. We were united as one, even though we were separate. I knew it had happened, but I didn't know what, if anything, I should do about it except just let it be and continue on with the healing work.

As I headed out, I stopped to talk with Nurse Sherrie. "What's going on with his kidneys? I thought they were doing better since he was producing urine and the bloating had gone down?"

She cleared her throat, pausing just long enough to let me know she didn't want to give bad news. "They're not fully functioning, I'm sorry to say." She hesitated, "While he's doing really well and he is making a miraculous recovery, it looks like there will be permanent kidney damage which will require lifelong dialysis or a transplant, if he's able to receive one, sometime down the road."

Undaunted, I replied, "Well, I guess we'll be doing extra work on his kidneys tomorrow!"

She looked at me like I was crazy, but I just laughed as though I was in on the joke that more could be done for his kidneys. After all, there were limits to energy work and the damage had been extensive. According to Sherrie and his doctors, the damage was irreversible.

But something in my spirit completely rebelled at that statement of defeat and I refused to give it another thought. In my mind, David had already experienced a huge miracle. He was alive. No one, except me, had believed that would happen. And, if he had one miracle, he could have another. I had absolute faith in God to pull this off, even if no one else believed it. I would not let my faith be dissuaded. I didn't know how I could believe any more than I already did, yet I left the hospital resolved to delve another layer deeper.

To begin with, I knew that due to the connection between us, I could work with him effectively remotely. We did not need to be in the same room. I had not considered having helpers, but later that night that's exactly what happened.

I'd like to be able to make sense of it all and say that I understand what happened next, but I can't, because it had not ever before, nor since, been a part of my background in healing. David and I had found a holistic portal of experience. Clearly, it was going to take something more than what God had been doing through me to bring David to a total recovery.

I stopped by Blockbuster on the way home, thinking I would rent something light. I decided to check out the campy movie my friend, Grace, had mentioned, *What the Bleep Do We Know?* It was filmed in Oregon, where Grace lived at the time, and had become an underground hit. Grace liked the concepts presented and had recommended it. I decided to rent the movie and see if I agreed. After all, some wild things were happening and it was clear I didn't know *what the bleep was going on,* either. Maybe the movie would have some enlightening views.

After I got home and settled, I popped the movie in and began to watch. The storyline, starring Marlee Matlin, was intriguing as were several metaphysical concepts presented in an entertaining and thought-provoking way. Now I was ready for bed.

I brushed my teeth and got into bed, thinking about David and his kidneys. I began to pray, but this time, I was feeling some doubt creep in. Maybe this had all been a fluke. Maybe he'd gotten more than anyone could hope for and should accept the healing he had received and just be grateful. But that conclusion didn't work too well for me. I felt there could be more, and I believed that God could do it.

"Dear God, I am asking for your help for David. I am asking you, God, and I am calling all the angels in the universe, and all the powers that are only the highest and best, the most sacred and holy, in all the dimensions, only of you, God, to help David. I believe you can restore his kidneys to total health. And I know you said that whatever we ask in your name, with faith, will be done. So, I am asking you God, to bring forth all your love and healing energy to help David. I give thanks and praise for the complete healing of his kidneys. In Jesus' name I pray, Amen."

I took a deep breath.

Quietude filled the room—a stillness almost like time had stopped. I became aware of David's eyes looking at me.

Then, the view switched and I was standing in his hospital room, observing the activity taking place. David was surrounded by four very tall beings who seemed to be a spiritual medical team. One was at his head, one at his feet, and one on each side. The one who seemed to be the team leader was clothed in blue scrubs. He was wearing a surgeon's cap and a facemask that extended below his chin. He stood on David's left side. His facial features were sharp—very prominent blue eyes and cheekbones, with narrow lips and a sharp, almost beak-like nose showing through the mask. He looked a little like a ghostly alien. The others were also wearing blue scrubs, caps, and facemasks. They appeared like any medical team, except that I could see through them. Although it was hard to distinguish their genders, it seemed there were two males and two females. Oddly enough, they were tinted blue, similar to the blue color of eastern Indian gods of enlightenment, such as Krishna. Apparently, God had heard my prayers and had sent a team of healing helpers.

The leader of the team was surgically repairing David's kidneys. One of the crew cradled David's head; the other held his feet. The remaining team member stood with his hands spread—one covering David's heart area and the other hovering over his lungs. I could sense they were all aware of me. The crew conferred telepathically with each other and with me. The lead healer paused, looked up at my astral presence, then looked away, letting me know he saw me but that he was still working. His movements were exceptionally crisp and fast. His bluish color made him look like a beamed projection from another dimension. They telepathically communicated that while I was away from David, they were working with him throughout the night.

I watched, fascinated, as the lead healer seemed to manifest a set of kidney, which seemed to float above David, as though suspended on an invisible tray. It was almost like the holographic organs were doppelgangers of the damaged ones. As I watched, the blue kidneys descended into David's body as if to replace the damaged ones.

When all was done, the lead doctor looked up and nodded at me, indicating that they had finished the regeneration.

The next thing I knew, I was back in my bed. I could not explain what had happened, except that I knew I had been out of my body and I was sure of those beings. I wondered if I was losing my mind.

The experience seemed vivid and real. Somehow, I had connected to the portal of another dimension. This portal had remained open so that they could come in and work to repair the physical body through the spirit body. I trusted that this was God's work. I fell into a deep sleep and woke in the morning to bright light streaming in through my bedroom window.

I got out of bed, though feeling ungrounded, and bumped into the night stand. The walls did not appear solid. I was off balance, feeling as if I was not yet completely in my physical body, as if I was floating.

On the way to the bathroom, I jammed my little toe on the door. I could feel it break. As the sharp pain shot through my toe, it began to turn purple and swell. I hobbled back to the bed and sat down, holding my injured foot. Now, I was definitely in my body and it hurt! I wrapped my hand around my toe, sending healing energy.

As my grogginess lifted I became more perplexed by what had happened the night before. Although I had never heard of this type of healing team and it seemed strange, it also jogged a memory that continued to elude me.

CHAPTER 14
ACCELERATED HEALING

Sunday, October 2, 2005

I didn't know if the blue healing team was a figment of my imagination or a waking dream. But when I got to the hospital, I could see something had changed with David. Although he was sleeping, he seemed to have improved overnight. His color was better and he looked more at peace. Nurse Sherrie said he'd had a rough night, which surprised me. I thought the healing team I'd envisioned would elicit a peaceful response, but if major things were happening, maybe not. "The feeding tube has been removed and he's now able to take small sips of water and a small bite of applesauce," she said.

I worked with David, saying the usual prayers and spending extra time hovering my hands over his kidney area. The energy was solidly vibrant today and I could feel it circulating through us both. I envisioned his kidneys full of living energy, healed, and whole. David hadn't woken up by the time I finished, so I quietly squeezed his hand and told him I'd be back the next day.

CHAPTER 15
EVERY KIND OF LOVE

Monday, October 3, 2005

Today in my Marriage and Family class we discussed the different types of love that people can experience. Love is one of those words that no one can ever quite define because it has so many complex expressions. I'd thought about the love I felt for my children, for previous loves in my life, for my family, my mom, my friends, for God. Each relationship had a completely different feeling, but they were all love in various forms.

The class was learning about the color wheel theory of love, developed by John Alan Lee, a Canadian psychologist, and described in his book, *Colours of Love: An Exploration of the Ways of Loving* (1973). Lee's model identified six main styles that included Eros (erotic/passion), Ludus (fun/playful), Storge (friendship/family), Mania (obsessive; a mix of Ludus and Eros), Pragma (practical, convenient), and Agape (pure love, altruistic). These six styles could be combined into nine styles with variations on the color wheel.

Lee was also an activist in the LGBT community in Canada, working on understanding the sociology of love for all people. He later came out as one of the first openly gay professional figures in 1974.[3] Given the earlier discussion the class had had about LGBT people and love, the understanding that love styles could be identified in a way that the students could apply to their own lives made sense to them.

And to me. Particularly since I was still trying to identify the type of love I'd experienced with David during our time together on the other side—this type of all-enveloping compassion that was so pure and clear, with nothing but understanding for the souls embraced in it, had no category. It was a paradox of emotion interpreted through my limited human understanding. I later described it as the "Every Kind of Love" style because it felt like the greatest love of all styles combined. And even these words didn't touch the quivering joy of that peaceful, loving light.

The days had flown by in a swirl and in between the extraordinary experiences I was having in working with David, my own life still had to be lived. Classes had to be taught, my kids needed care and attention. Still, though, I had been thinking about David's mother, Dee. I hadn't heard from her and didn't have her phone number. I knew she'd been hearing that David was improving, but I didn't know if she knew that I was continuing my visits. I felt a bond with her that I didn't understand and for some reason, I wanted her to know that I was helping her son as I'd offered to do. I wasn't sure what I expected her to say or what I wanted to hear, but I wanted to make that connection.

Later that day, I went to see David. He was awake now but still not able to talk. He smiled at me when I came in, and he reached out his arms to me for a hug. David's roommate, Sean, was there. Sean was a nursing student and an all-around sweet man. He stood over six feet tall, had large

---

[3]   https://en.wikipedia.org/wiki/John_Alan_Lee

glasses, a shiny bald head with some fringe, and a big boyish grin. He talked with a strong New York accent that his years in Virginia had not changed.

Dee called while Sean was there. I was holding David's hand and standing there feeling the peace and energy flow through us. After Sean gave an update, he handed the phone over to me, saying that Dee wanted to talk to me.

"Hello, Scarlett."

I said hello back, feeling awkward and not sure what to say.

"Sean said David is doing much better and that you've been there each day."

"Yes, that's right. David's made an amazing recovery. The doctors and nurses here are calling him 'Miracle Boy.' "

"Well, we've been praying for him and so have the people in my AA group. On our last visit there, David's brother, Stephen, laid his hands on David and I could feel a powerful connection between them. I think that's what saved David."

"No doubt that everyone's love and prayers have brought him to where he is now," I said. "I'm certain he wouldn't be here without that. But I wanted you to know that I have been coming every day and I am doing all I can to help him, just like I said I would. It's been an amazing experience to see him recover."

"Well, thank you for being there for him. And for me. It means more than I can say," Dee said. "Today is Rosh Hashanah," she added.

"Can you tell me more about that?"

"It's the Jewish New Year where each person's fate for the coming year is written into the Book of Life."

"It seems David is getting a second chance for the New Year," I said.

As I was talking with Dee, I felt that same presence of peace and love that I'd felt when I worked with David. I could feel a sense of connection with Dee. She felt like a mother to me, and I felt such love for her and from her. I later came to see that most people felt that way about her. She radiated love, peace, acceptance, and wisdom. I wanted her to be happy and I wanted to help her. I was glad that her son was healing and grateful to be able to help in any way I could. Dee and I said our goodbyes after assuring each other we'd stay in touch.

I was thinking about what she'd said about everyone's prayers. It didn't mean that I wasn't doing anything and I didn't feel any sense of ego around it. Yet I knew that my presence there was making a difference and that it was critical for some understanding that I was doing the energy connection. I viewed myself as a healing facilitator. When I was working with David, I felt the love and prayers of others flow through me as though I were a conductor of that collective love. I didn't know any other way to describe what was happening.

After Sean left, I began with prayers and then the energy exchange with David. I felt the energy flowing through us. I was abuzz with it. My left hand was hovering over his kidneys and my right hand was moving back and forth so fast it was blurring. Then it just stopped. My hand was still and the energy left. David had fallen asleep and I was glad of that. He needed to rest to absorb it all. I kissed him on the forehead and quietly left the room.

When I got home, Greg called to check in. I'd been so caught up in everything I barely noticed that we hadn't talked. I told Greg what was going on and he said he was glad that David was doing better. I was aware that I didn't have romantic feelings for David because the love was so powerful, yet I didn't know how to interpret it. It felt sacred and holy, not romantic. But I did have romantic feelings for Greg and was hoping we might get a chance now to explore them.

As intuitive as I was with others, and despite the transcendent experiences I was having with David, I was having a hard time understanding what was going on with Greg. He seemed interested but distant, which confused me.

I was able to apply what I was learning and teaching in class, though, and it was becoming clear that Greg might be interested in playing and having fun but I was more interested in love and commitment. Greg was tall and athletic, with a handsome face and twinkling blue eyes. He was trying to get his business off the ground and I would share marketing tips with him. We had an unusual friendship developing, and a bond of recovery, too. Greg was funny, with a quick wit that made me laugh. But he clearly had some things to work through and it was becoming more evident to me that we would probably not make it romantically. Still, I liked him and was willing to see where things went.

Chapter 16

Relapse

Tuesday, October 4, 2005

Over the next few days, David's recovery was swift. But then he had a setback. While his lungs and kidneys seemed to be doing better, his brain was getting deprived of blood by the vessels shutting off the supply.

I asked the nurses if they had headphones so we could put music on to keep his brain stimulated. I brought my Kenny Loggins CD, *The Unimaginable Life*, and thought the gentle yet inspirational music would be healing for him. I played Steven Halpern's *Crystal Healing* CD and my Reiki CDs. Frank and Sean also brought some hard rock, saying David liked that, too.

I felt a sense of panic course through me. I didn't want David to go. We'd still never talked, yet I felt a connection to him and felt such a great love. Was that the lesson? That love is a force all its own and it comes and goes like a light switch flicked on and off? I felt selfish and attached. I said my prayers and asked God to guide us and to help me with my feelings. I couldn't be selfish because whatever happened was not up to me. This really was between David and God.

During the next few days I came twice a day, once in the morning and then again in the evening. In between playing Guns 'N Roses, Kenny Loggins, and Reiki, along with prayers and healing energy, David pulled through.

CHAPTER 17
HIGH HOLY DAYS

Wednesday - Thursday, October 5 - 6

It seemed it was spiritually significant that David was going through this during the Jewish holy days. They seemed to influence David's recovery and indicate that he was being given a new start.

I talked to my friend Dr. Esther Roth, who advised me on the sacredness of Jewish traditions. Esther had come from Romania and Israel and was a psychologist who had become a tremendously successful financial advisor. Esther and I had become friends after she was referred to me for a health consultation during a period when she was recovering from cancer. I had taken an exam for my Certified Health Education Specialist designation (CHES) after finishing my master's degree in public health and thus had studied the role of nutrition with a focus on essential fatty acids, especially omega-3's found in fish oils. My master's thesis was in the Library of Congress and I was sure that was going to be my career path. I had set up my business, the Healing Connection, to provide nutritional education and energy healing to help people, including my own children—who were both doing better, it seemed.

I met with Esther to talk about what was happening with David. I was worried that the experiences I was having would strike her as crazy, but she took them seriously and even seemed to find them normal. She understood mysticism and had also experienced things she couldn't explain after the death of her beloved husband. She felt his presence with her and accepted it without batting an eye.

Esther was also the one who got me started on learning about how to manage money and encouraged me to go for my Ph.D. in public policy. She showed me how to leverage the equity in my condo and, along with the stipend I received for the Ph.D., how to quit my job so I could go to school full time and still pay my bills. She taught me more about money than anyone else ever had and to this day, I am grateful for her brilliance and advice.

During the next few days, David's progress was rapid and astonishing. He was increasingly more alert and when I came in on Wednesday early afternoon, Frank was there. He told me that David had talked earlier, saying a few words in response to the nurse's questions, including asking David what was the last book he remembered reading. I thought that was a strange thing to ask someone but the nurses had been informed that David was an avid reader and had even brought a book with him to the ER when he came there thinking he was only having a panic attack.

David told the nurse he was reading about Thomas Jefferson, and that was accurate. David had glasses on now. I didn't know he wore glasses but it helped his eyes look more focused. He was still very shaky and weak but he seemed better. I was pleased to hear he was a reader. I usually read three books at a time for fun, in addition to my research reading, so I definitely appreciated that he was a reader, too. I wasn't sure why I cared at the time, but I did.

David didn't talk when I was there, and I was feeling a little disappointed because I was curious what his voice sounded like. I was coming twice a day, so I thought I would hear his voice that evening if he was up to talking.

I asked Frank if he'd like to stay while I worked with David. Normally I preferred to be alone with David to keep the energy flowing without anyone else's mixing in, but Frank was and is such a sweet person that I felt it would be fine if he stayed.

"I don't know what to do," Frank said.

"Just keep praying and keep holding his hand. That's all I need you to do. Let's start with the Lord's Prayer."

David was looking at me and Frank was standing there looking like he felt uncomfortable. I felt self-conscious and awkward. I closed my eyes and focused on God and love and healing and David. Then the peace and love started to flow and the energy in the room zoomed in, charged with Frank's presence.

"Our Father, which art in heaven, hallowed be thy name," Frank and I said together. "Thy kingdom come, thy will be done, on earth as it is in heaven." The power of the words we were saying and their true meaning rained over me with their energy. "On earth AS IT IS in heaven." It struck me that the words we were saying meant that what was on earth was a reflection of how it actually was in heaven. In heaven, David *was* healed. His earthly body was merely catching up to that fact.

Frank and I continued the prayer. "Give us this day our daily bread and forgive us our trespasses as we forgive those who trespass against us. And lead us not into temptation but deliver us from evil. For thine is the kingdom, the power, and the glory, for ever and ever. Amen."

I waved my hands over David's body, scanning and assessing how his energy felt—it felt clear and good. I had brought organic sesame oil with me to put at various reflexology points on his feet. I also brought lavender and eucalyptus essential oils to put under his nose and on his pillow, if he liked the scent.

I spent extra time working on David's feet, massaging the toes, and pressing the oil into the soft part of his upper foot and then into his heels. I remember reading that people who had had near-death experiences reported slipping out of their body through their feet. I hoped the sesame oil, in addition to the healing properties of the omega-6 fatty acids, could also help provide a seal to his energy field, which still felt porous. Nevertheless, his energy was stronger and more vibrant than it had been before and the flow was surrounding all three of us in a peaceful and radiant way.

When I finished the session, I refocused my attention on Frank. He was standing there, still holding David's hand, with his eyes closed and a smile on his face. David was asleep.

In a soft tone, I asked Frank if he could feel the energy. He said he didn't know the words to describe it, but he felt something. Frank has a strong Southern accent and speaks simply and plainly. Feeling "something" without elaboration was probably the most Frank would say about it. He seemed peaceful, though.

I said I was headed home and would be back later. I asked Frank if he was coming back, and he said he wasn't sure about tonight but he'd be back tomorrow. I gave him a hug, squeezed David's hand, and left.

That evening when I went back to the hospital, I was pleasantly surprised to find David awake and sitting up. His glasses were on and he seemed focused and alert. He looked at me, still unable to say anything. I had brought my tuning forks with me because I felt that the vibration of them would be useful in calibrating the energy field around David's kidneys.

Before I did the prayers and because David was seemingly more alert than I had ever seen him be, I asked, "Can you talk?" He shook his head as if to say no, and pointed to his throat. I nodded and said, "We'll continue to work on your throat. Right now, I'm going to focus on your kidneys. Is that ok?" He nodded yes. Soon after I started, he seemed to tire and fell asleep.

I used the tuning forks, hovering them over his kidneys and lungs and then waving them around his body. The buzz of the forks filled the room and I could feel the whole vibration change. I felt a shift within David and me.

I held his hands again and prayed out loud for his healing, for the highest and best to happen for him, and for peace and love to guide him from this moment forward. When I closed the prayer, I felt such compassion for him over the confusion, sadness, and hurt he was surely feeling. I didn't know what had happened in his life but I knew there had been much pain. I also knew God could heal anything. David was living proof.

I brought out the essential oils and dabbed some lavender in the middle of his forehead and under his nose and on his throat, along with putting some on his pillow. He briefly stirred but remained asleep.

I leaned over and whispered to David, "The portal is closed. You're back. You'll be on your feet tomorrow." I spoke with certainty even when I didn't understand why I was using the word "portal" or how I could know that he would be able to stand. But I knew that his healing was moving forward with great strides.

The thought came to me, "You can take it from here." I didn't know if that was a whisper from God, but the truth struck me that I would be connecting with David more than I had imagined possible.

CHAPTER 18
MY TRUE, LOVING COMPANION

Friday, October 7, 2005

I had been in touch with a Unity minister online whom I'd asked for prayer.[4] I had read his online posts about healing, love, prosperity and all the topics that interested me as a struggling single mom. He had been kind to me and had sent me writings about finding my true, loving companion that God had chosen for me. I was thinking about our correspondence that morning and reflecting on the positive affirmations I had learned as a member of a prayer team for a Unity church.

I was also thinking about the Reiki work I was doing and the powerful dimensions that I had experienced through it in my work with others and now with David. I had completed my Reiki mastership in April of 2005 after seven years of study. My Reiki master/teacher, was an amazing woman. When we did the level three attunements, my body shook from head to toe, having flooded with the love I used to feel as a child, much as I felt when I was baptized in holy spirit. I could not contain the love that was flowing into me while

---

[4] Rev. John Adams, The Golden Key Ministry: http://www.goldenkeyministry.com/

doing those final attunements; the love was so strong that tears of joy were streaming.

Now, working with David had opened the door to that pure, unfettered love that shook me to the core, just like the attunements had.

Memories of times I experienced that love came rushing back, including when I felt the Holy Spirit in the Baptist church I went to with my grandparents as a child and would sing joyfully about God's love. When I went to youth group at another Baptist church and could feel love all around me. When I was baptized in the Holy Spirit at a Pentecostal church I'd gone to when I was 16.

When I worked with others, I felt that same love and compassion surround us.

I began to connect the spiritual dots and see that there were no separations in spirit. Whether it was through Unity, a Pentecostal religion, Reiki, or a Baptist church, it didn't matter. God was love and love was the connector of it all. Love was all that mattered. And somehow that love could flow through me and into others. It was a sacred gift and I was grateful for it.

Later that day I was back at the hospital, gazing at David while he slept. I was thinking about his life and wondering what had gone so wrong for him. I couldn't make sense of my feeling that I was meant to be with him, especially given how sick he still was and how I didn't really know him or about the life he had lived that had led him to this point. I was confused by what I was feeling on one level, and on another, the love was just there and my mind couldn't talk me out of it. Feeling tired and overwhelmed, I left the room and went downstairs to get a quick lunch and think.

When I got back to his room, he was still sleeping, so I sat in a chair and rested and thought my prayers to him, just waiting for him to wake up. When he opened his eyes he looked disoriented. His eyes weren't focused and he looked afraid. The nurses had told me out in the hallway before I came in that he'd had a breathing treatment and it had not gone well.

I got up from the chair, took his hands and held them in mine for quite a while. He looked into my eyes and I looked into his. Abruptly, he took his hands away and put them over his head, turned his head to the side and wouldn't look at me. I was startled by his sudden withdrawal and didn't know what to do, but I understood that he was feeling something and he needed time to himself.

"David, it seems my work is pretty much done, but I could come see you later if you want me to."

He just lay there listless and unresponsive.

I left feeling strangely sad as though the energy had cut off and now there was no connection. I went home and called my mother to ask for advice. She said it wasn't unusual for patients to have negative reactions in the ICU. I told her how disoriented he seemed and that he had had a breathing treatment and she informed me about ICU psychosis and that it could have been part of what was going on.

Mom also suggested I take the weekend off and rest up, which I did.

I called David on Sunday to see how he was doing and talked to him on the phone. I asked him if he would like me to come visit again. "Yes," he said, his voice sounding tired. "Yes, just not today since I haven't had a chance to get cleaned up."

"Okay. I'll come tomorrow if that's okay with you."

"Yes, I want to see you."

Feeling relieved, I said goodbye and visualized sending him loving energy to surround him.

Chapter 19

Release

Monday, October 10, 2005

Today's Marriage and Family class topic covered how alcohol, drugs, and other addictions could impact marriages, families, and relationships. This topic hit a nerve with nearly everyone. I was surprised by how many students and their families were impacted by addiction. I shared some of my background about growing up with alcoholism and its impact on me and the recovery efforts I had made to move forward in my life. I had a guest speaker that day named Nathan, who was a rehab counselor. He was also a dear friend who was in recovery for his own issues and worked with adolescents who were struggling too.

The students were sharing their stories about alcohol and other drugs, talking about their families, and how their brothers and sisters were struggling and the devastating consequences to so many people, including themselves. The same questions kept coming up. How can I fix this? How can I help them? Is it my fault? How do you know if you have a problem?

"What's so bad about addiction?" Nathan asked the class. The room was silent. "C'mon, anyone? I've got something for the first person who says something!"

One of the students said, " 'Cause it sucks?"

The class laughed and Nathan threw him a piece of candy.

"First prize goes to the young man in row five! You're right, man, addiction sucks. You know why? Because addiction takes away your freedom to choose. Once the booze or drugs hits your system, they're in charge. You're sure as hell not, am I right?"

The room erupted in laughter. The students began to ask more questions. Nathan told them how addiction progressed. Generally, things start out as fun at parties. Then, during the fun, problems begin to happen. Finally, there's no fun at all, only problems. Addiction is like a craving that has to be fed and the person has no choice left but to feed the addiction monster. It's taken over, costing a person their health and even their life as the addiction makes their choices for them. He talked about some of the related issues for college students, such as driving drunk, failing in classes, date rape, overdoses, and death.

"Addiction is selfish, right? It doesn't care who gets hurt or who dies. It doesn't care that everyone you love is hurt by your behavior. All the love in the world won't fix it. That's why we call it a disease. It's a sickness that takes over your body, mind, and spirit and you get swallowed up by it. And everyone around you suffers."

I could tell his words were opening the minds and eyes of many of my students who had not heard addiction talked about in this way.

"It's insanity to keep doing something that hurts you and those you love over and over and over, yes? No sane person would do this to themselves, would they? But that's what addiction is. It's insanity. It's crazy."

Nathan shared his recovery story and explained that he was an active member of a 12-step recovery program, Alcoholics Anonymous, for his own former drinking days.

He wrote his contact info on the board and told the class if anyone needed help or wanted to talk, to call him or shoot him an email. The class ended and I thanked Nathan for coming and sharing his humor, honesty, and effective communication style with the students.

One of my students named Clarissa was standing there waiting as I said goodbye to Nathan. An African-American woman in her late 20s or early 30s, with long braids, a sweet, full face and a quiet demeanor, she'd rarely spoken in class. She wanted to thank me, she said, and wanted to talk to me about her mother's alcoholism and her sister's drug addiction. She said she felt guilty and ashamed that she couldn't seem to help them. She was the first of her family to go to college and she was working part-time to support herself and her young daughter. Her sister was addicted to meth and had five kids that she could barely take care of. She would ask Clarissa for money and she would give what she could because she felt sorry for the kids.

In response, I told her about Al-Anon, a 12-step program to help family members cope with their loved ones' addictions by focusing on their own spiritual connection and recovery. I told her the three C's of the program: you didn't cause it, you can't cure it, and you can't control it. Relief crossed her face and then she started to cry.

"What's wrong, Clarissa?"

"I'm so angry! I hate her. I hate them both!" She was sobbing now. "And I'm so ashamed of myself for feeling that way. I know I should feel sorry for them and I do, but I hate them for wrecking their lives and for hurting me too. I'm ashamed that I'm so selfish."

"Oh Clarissa, you're not selfish! Of course you would feel like that! It's normal and healthy to feel that way! Why wouldn't you?"

"It is?" she asked, looking surprised.

"Yes, it is. You're in pain and so are they. Here's the thing: addiction is a force all its own and it's ruining their lives and they can't stop it. And neither can you. I think that's what you hate, is that right?"

Clarissa nodded.

"But you love them, right?"

Clarissa nodded again.

"Can you understand that you can love the person and hate the addiction?"

"Um, yeah," Clarissa said slowly, and I could tell she was thinking over this idea.

"Yes, I can see that! I'm still angry but I can see that I love them. I'm just so hurt by it all and I don't know how to help," she paused and took a deep breath.

"I wish sometimes they would just die. I can't believe I am telling you this," she said, looking away from me, fearing that I would judge her or express shock.

I felt that sense of compassionate love from the other side surround us, like a cocoon gently embracing us. The room was still and we were fully connected as soulful beings in a healing encounter. I took her hand.

"It's normal to want an end to suffering, Clarissa, for them and for you. It's okay to feel how you're feeling. You're not alone."

Her face relaxed and she stopped crying. "Thank you," she said softly.

We exchanged hugs and I told her we could talk more later if she wanted. I could see she was feeling better and that something inside had shifted for her. She had another class to go to and I had a visit to David to make.

When I got to the hospital, David was awake and alert. He seemed distant though. He didn't reach out his arms for a hug. We were strangers after all. He said he was able to eat solid food today for the first time.

"I'm craving barbeque," he said. "I think Frank and the guys are going to bring some later."

"That sounds great! If they don't, just let me know and I'll bring you some tomorrow."

"Thank you. I don't know where I'm going tomorrow. The doctor said I'm doing so much better that I'm going to a different unit."

"So how are you feeling?"

"I'm feeling okay. I just don't know what's happened to me or what's going to happen next."

I took his hand. "Whatever happens next, you're going to be okay."

David's eyes met mine and I felt that floating feeling which made me seem like I'd drift up from my chair without moving a muscle. I heard the door open and in walked Jack, whom I had heard about. Jack is an African-American man who was in AA with David, and he and David had developed a strong bond before David became ill.

"How's my brother from a different mother?" Jack's booming laugh filled the room. Jack's wide grin was contagious and he exuded warm, loving energy. This was my first time meeting him but I'd heard about him from Frank. When Jack wanted to visit David initially, the hospital wouldn't let him in because he wasn't family. However, David's mother, on her first visit, said that Jack was her son so they let him make regular visits. I liked him instantly.

I introduced myself.

"Oh, I know who you are, Miss Lady. I heard how you helped my brother here."

"Well, God did all the work, Jack."

"Yeah, through you."

"We all did what we could. David's lucky to have so many people who love him. I'm going to head out and let you guys visit. David, I'll check in later." I gave David's hand a gentle squeeze, hugged Jack and left.

CHAPTER 20
MEETING DAVID

Tuesday, October 11, 2005

Jackie and I had plans for lunch after the criminal justice class in which I was a teaching assistant ended. When we met, I was filling her in on how things had been going with David. I told her I had called him last night and checked to see if he got the barbeque he was craving. That he had told me that they didn't bring it last night but might tonight. I said if it didn't work out, "I make a good barbequed chicken and could bring that to you."

The conversation shifted from our personal lives back to our Ph.D. programs. Jackie was struggling with the economics class. I could relate because it was all I could do to get through it too. I had not had economics in my undergraduate classes so to have my first introduction to it be at the Ph.D. level was daunting. But the basic concepts of supply, demand, and scarcity made sense to me. I certainly understood about scarcity from being a single mother, college student, and adjunct faculty. More supply than demand meant prices go down. Less supply with more demand meant prices go up. Achieving equilibrium or balance was the goal when possible. When I thought about it in terms of energy and healing, it made sense even more. Everything had a flow to it including our economic system and our bodies. We were all subject to invisible forces, such as Adam Smith's invisible hand, that guided the marketplace and perhaps even humanity.

But the charts and graphs as they were initially explained by our professor confused us both. When I took the class, we were required to write a 20-page paper on an economics topic. My paper was on the cost savings of addressing mental health issues holistically. With all that I'd gone through with my boys in researching the role of omega-3 and -6 fatty acids in ADHD and epilepsy, I knew there were better approaches to explore in addition to some of the standard treatments. I had been a key presenter at the National Alliance on Mental Illness (NAMI) annual conference on the role of nutrition and its impact on mental illness and its potential to help those who were suffering, along with their families. My conclusion was that better nutrition would ultimately save money and improve lives and that an integrative approach would work better.

Our conversation drifted again when Jackie asked how things were going with Greg.

"I don't know. I haven't really heard much from him. I called him the other day and asked if he wanted to go visit David with me, but he said he couldn't. What do you make of that?"

"Do you think that Greg showed up so he could lead you to David?"

I thought about that, not quite sure how I felt about it all. "Well, if you mean to help David, sure, I guess."

"Maybe you and David are meant to be together."

"C'mon, Jackie, are you crazy? There's nothing for me and David. I'm sure I was supposed to help him, but he has a really long road ahead. Besides, I don't have romantic feelings for him."

"You love him though," Jackie said, almost factually.

I hesitated, then: "It's true I love him but it's a different kind of love. Maybe he and I can do some healing work together when he gets back on his feet and we can help others with that love."

Jackie laughed. "Uh huh. Yeah. That's it."

"He's not my type! That's not what this is about. Maybe there's some karma here. But I think it's more about expanding my abilities as a healer."

"Alright, 'Miss Thing.' We'll see what happens next," she laughed more.

When I got to my car, I noticed a message showing on my phone. I hadn't heard it ring. It was David. I was surprised to see he had my number, but I remembered I had left him my card. He wanted to know if my offer was still on to bring the barbequed chicken. I called him back and told him I'd be by at six that night. "Great!" he excitedly replied. "Oh, and I've been transferred to a step-down room. I'm in room 450 now."

"Don't worry. I'll find you."

Then I went to the store and quickly got back home to cook. A few hours later I packaged up the barbequed chicken, mashed potatoes, peas, and warm banana muffins I'd just made. Comfort food would probably be welcomed.

When I got there, David held his arms out for a hug and he was looking so much healthier, and more handsome. His hair was combed and his eyes, brown and soft, were looking deeply into mine.

He was still shaky and fairly weak; it seemed to me he was also quite tired. We made small talk for a while and I asked him if he wanted to eat now. He did, so I laid out the food. I could tell he felt a little self-conscious, so I told him I was going to head home and let him relax. I left wondering what kind of love I was feeling for him.

Chapter 21
Making the Connections

Wednesday, October 12, 2005

The Marriage and Family class focused today on date rape and the issues surrounding it. The topic tied in with the previous class in highlighting the correlation with alcohol and other drugs often being factors in these violent crimes. The class discussion was intense. Now that the group realized we could talk about any topic with respect for everyone's views, the students didn't hold back.

I had a meeting after my class with the Job Corps office in Richmond. Job Corps is a free training program that helps kids like Ryan get an education and training for a career. I was trying to find a program for my son that might help him with needed job skills and wanted to find out more about what was involved and whether he would even qualify. He was struggling in school and it didn't seem that he was going in a good direction, so the program looked like a good fit. But we would need to apply, visit the center in West Virginia, wait to see if they would accept him, and if so, hope Ryan would stick with it.

David called later that afternoon to tell me he was going to be discharged to a local rehabilitation facility in a few days. "I need a walker because my legs are still very weak. But I'll have physical therapy and be there until I'm strong enough to go home. They plan to send me there on Saturday." Today was Wednesday.

He said he still couldn't comprehend that it had been less than a week since he'd regained consciousness. Thinking it over, I realized that by this coming Friday it would be three weeks since I began working with him. In two and a half weeks he had gone from lung and kidney failure, possible brain damage, double pneumonia, sepsis, cardiac arrhythmia, a month-long coma, using a respirator, dialysis, and feeding tube to stay alive, to near-death, to being fully alive.

"I loved the barbeque you brought me last night, except I wasn't able to eat as much as I would have liked. I'm still trying to get my appetite back."

I was enjoying just listening to his happy voice.

"Did I tell you I don't need dialysis anymore?"

"No, I didn't know that."

"The doctor said my kidneys are fully functioning. They don't know how they are, but they are."

"Wow, that's amazing, David!"

The image of the blue healing team flashed into my mind. I knew there would come a time when I would share this experience with David, but now wasn't it.

"Are you hurting anywhere?" I asked.

"Not really. I get winded pretty fast when I try to do things like walk and I'm still pretty weak. But man, I'm just grateful I'm alive."

"Well, I'll let you rest up. I'll come by Friday to pick up my CD player if that's ok with you."

"Yes, that sounds good. Maybe we can chat tomorrow," David said.

"Okay, sure, that would be great. Call me anytime."

Afterwards I sat there for a moment thinking about how with the extensive damage and the poor prognosis he'd been given, having both fully functioning kidneys now seemed like a real miracle.

CHAPTER 22
DAY OF ATONEMENT

Thursday, October 13, 2005

Today was Yom Kippur, the Day of Atonement, one of the most important holidays of the Jewish year. The central themes involve atoning for one's mistakes and repenting. While Dee had explained to me that according to Jewish tradition God inscribes each person's fate for the coming year into the Book of Life on Rosh Hashanah, Yom Kippur is the day to seal the decree.

I talked with David briefly that evening. He said he was feeling better but just very tired. I reminded him I'd come see him the next day. We talked briefly about it being Yom Kippur and what that meant to him. He said that he felt forgiven and knew that he had some work to do to make amends as he got better.

I remembered how I could sense David's feelings of guilt and shame when we were in that place together. I could also feel the loving, compassionate force that forgave all. It seemed that David's fate was sealed and he would recover completely. He had been given his second chance. What would he do with it?

Chapter 23

The Healing Continues

Friday, October 14, 2005

I headed to the hospital that evening and arrived at around 7:45. I brought six small packets of Vitamin C with me with the intention of chatting briefly, grabbing my CD player, and then leaving. I felt nervous around him and awkward—it was so hard to have that level of connection with someone, such soulful intimacy, and then to be meeting each other as strangers in real life.

When I got there, I anxiously grabbed the CD player and handed him the Vitamin C packets. Then I sat next to him and he reached out his hand. When our hands connected, all of the awkwardness I had felt melted away and in its place I felt the whoosh of love circling around us. David said how overwhelmed he was with the outpouring of love from so many. He said he felt bathed in the love of everyone's prayers. He asked if I could tell him about what I had done when I was working with him.

I told him about the energy work I'd done and the prayers that I'd said. "I talked directly to your organs."

"Oh!? Well, looks like it worked," he said and laughed.

I mentioned Reiki, the tuning forks, foot rubs, organic sesame oil, the reflexology points on his feet, the music, and all the energy that was around us. I told him I had never experienced that much energy flowing in and around and that it was powerfully filled with a force I can only call love, for lack of a better word.

I told him how as he became more conscious, he would show me what he wanted. For example, the day he turned on his side and indicated for me to rub his back and the day he took my hand and put it to his throat.

"I don't remember any of that except for the foot rub. And feeling loved."

He then told me that today the doctors had found some blood clots in his arm. And that his back was hurting.

"Do you want me to do some energy work?" I asked.

"Yes. Would you please?"

David settled back and closed his eyes. As I held his hand, I moved my other hand up to his arm. I could feel the little clots and I envisioned them dissolving. In the earlier days when he was unconscious, I would have spoken to them, but now I felt self-conscious. Instead, I focused on visualizing them all healed. Then I moved my hands, which by now were hot, and placed one under the small of his back. I could feel the energy buzzing through my hand and radiating into his body.

Then the energy stopped just as it always did when finished. David opened his eyes and we sat there, holding hands and talking for the next hour. We talked about him being in the hospital in the coma during the Jewish holidays. It seemed significant to me that he was having these experiences during this deeply spiritual time.

We talked about him being Jewish and I told him I followed what Christ taught. I told him more about Reiki and how it was not religious, but rather how it worked with the universal life energy that we all have. I told him about the love that was there for him and that it was so huge it was impossible to express. I told him he was in it and that I was there with him in it.

He nodded. "I know. I don't know how I know, but I know."

His hands were shaky, so I knew he needed some of the omega-6 essential fatty acids. "Would you like me to rub your feet with sesame oil?"

"I'd like that," he said.

While I was putting the oil on his feet and pressing on his heels, I told him about my research into nutrition and the immune system. "You'll need to rebuild your immune system with extra vitamin B-complex, zinc, vitamin C, and essential fatty acids."

"I know a bit about nutrition, but not about fatty acids. What are they?"

"You've heard of fish oil, right? That's called an omega-3 fatty acid. I know you don't want a nutrition lesson now, but we can talk more about it as you get better if you want. It will really help speed up your recovery."

He reminded me that he was transferring to the rehab place, Sheltering Arms, the next day. "I'll call you in a few days when I get settled in." He smiled and squeezed my hand as he wished me a good night.

On the way home I had a strong feeling, really more of a knowing, that David was going to be okay.

CHAPTER 24
GOING HOME

Monday, October 17, 2005

I didn't hear from David over the weekend. Then on Monday afternoon he called. "I'm home."

"They didn't keep you at Sheltering Arms?" I was surprised.

"I didn't go at all," he said. "The doctor came in Saturday morning and examined me and said I was doing so much better that I didn't need to go. He said he was sending me home instead."

"That's great!"

"Yes, it really is. I'm not sure what you did, but it made a difference."

"Well, thanks for letting me know. It was the foot rub," I laughed. "If you want another, let me know."

"Okay, I will."

While I kept him in my prayers, I felt that I would need to move on. My healing work was done and he was going to be alright. He needed to focus on his recovery and also on making amends for whatever he had earlier alluded to that had gone wrong. I felt sad to let go because there seemed to be a lingering bond. What was the nature of it? Was it just because we'd had the shared near-death experience? I knew people reported feeling that indescribable love. So maybe that kind of universal love was there but it just wasn't personal. Whatever love it was, it called for wanting the best for David and that's all I needed to focus on.

CHAPTER 25
HOME VISIT

Tuesday, October 18, 2005

I was feeling restless, so I met Frank for coffee and then we went on to dinner. We talked about David and how well he was doing. Frank said he didn't think David was going to make it until I started working with him. "I don't know what you did, but whatever it was, it helped."

I told him that I was glad to have done whatever I could to contribute to David's healing. I knew the amazing doctors and nurses who took care of David had all done their parts, and that everyone's prayers and visits made a huge difference too. "Especially yours, Frank. You've been there every day for David. What an incredible friend you've been. He's very lucky to have you."

"It's what we do. We help each other," he said, referring to the fellowship of AA. "Why don't you come with me to visit David now?"

"No, I don't think it makes sense. I don't need to get to know him any further. What's the point? My work is done and he needs to get on with his life."

"I think it would be good for you to be friends. You really helped him a lot and he'd probably like to see you. Let's go grab a pie and take it to him."

The grocery store was in the same shopping center, so we walked over and got David a chocolate pie. I followed Frank over to David's. Sean greeted us at the door and led us back to the den where David was sitting, looking through his stacks of mail.

His face lit up when he saw us, especially when we said we'd brought one of his favorite pies. I noticed that David's hands were very shaky and that he still seemed quite weak, as well as distracted. Even so, to my surprise, he said he planned on attending our AA meeting the next night. Then he added, "My brother is coming to visit so maybe someone there will have some extra sheets and blankets to loan us."

Frank looked at me. "Scarlett, do you have any you could lend?"

"Sure. I'll drop them off at the meeting tomorrow night."

As I listened to David get caught up on politics and what was going on in the world, I was impressed with his intelligence and insight. Without warning, I felt a yawning sense of loss. I remembered the love that was surrounding us when we were in that dimension together and yearned to be back in it. With him. But that was me being selfish, and he had his own life to fix. Feeling uncomfortable, I said goodbye and headed home.

CHAPTER 26

BACK ON HIS FEET

Thursday, October 20, 2005

That night I went to the meeting at the same church where I'd met David's mother. I had packed the sheets, blanket, and pillow in my car. David said he was going to try to come, but I wasn't sure he'd be well enough to make it.

Then, just as the meeting was about to start, David arrived, slowly pushing along on his walker while leaning heavily on it. Sean and Frank flanked him until he made it to the table. Everyone cheered. David thanked everyone for their prayers and support. The meeting went on as usual and then we were all getting ready to leave.

David hadn't made much eye contact with me, so I walked over to him to say hello and tell him I had the bed items he wanted to borrow. "I'll grab them from my car." He had ridden with Sean, so I gave them to him to put in the trunk. As I was leaving, David said "thank you" and then held out his arms for a quick hug. Worried he might lose his balance, we hugged for just a moment. The awkwardness I had felt before, that I thought had been washed away, returned.

CHAPTER 27
BACK IN THE REAL WORLD

Wednesday, October 26, 2005

The week flew by. I had arranged for a guest speaker for my Marriage and Family class who was going to perform a one-woman play on domestic violence. She had written the play to educate others about the dangers of domestic violence and to help her heal from the death of her own sister, who had been killed by her abusive boyfriend. As she acted out how the violent boyfriend called her sister names like bitch and whore, and how he slapped, kicked, and punched her, the class sat silent. Several of the students had tears streaming down their faces, not even bothering to wipe them away. The actress played all of the parts and her performance was mesmerizing. She had begged her sister to leave and her family had tried everything, but her sister kept going back, again and again, with the abuse increasing, until the boyfriend finally shot her dead. The power of the acting and the message left the class and me stunned.

Many of the students talked about domestic violence in their own lives and the horror of those experiences, having seen too many loved ones victimized. The unhealthy glue between the abuser and the abused baffled most of the students. We talked about the cycle of abuse and how the victims get pulled into it. We talked about how even the worst people have something to love within them and that's what keeps the abused person hooked.

Many of the male students said they couldn't understand why women kept going back after they'd been beaten. We talked about men who were abused, too, although about 85 percent of victims were women. Abuse included physical, emotional, verbal, mental, sexual, and financial abuse, to name a few. Keeping women trapped, unable to work, isolated and cornered were often reasons why women couldn't leave. Even if they wanted to, they didn't have access to money. They'd been so beaten down they'd lost perspective and often didn't want to leave, believing things could change for the better.

I took my guest to lunch after the class and thanked her profusely for her courage in sharing her story and for her artistry in communicating it in a way that statistics never could.

When I got home later that day, I found my mood was low. I had been profoundly shaken by the class and the performance. I had experienced some awful things in my previous relationships, too, which is one reason why I had not wanted to date for a while. I needed time to work on me and to heal. I didn't trust that I knew enough to be able to choose wisely. Clearly, I had made bad choices, so it was better to just let it go and be alone. I was tired of being hurt. I had really liked Greg, but nothing was working out there.

I thought about the love that I had experienced with David in that dimension I couldn't even name. Why, I wondered, couldn't we humans experience that kind of love, if only just a bit of it? Why were people suffering so much in relationships? Why were people so cruel to one another? Why did people act as though love meant owning another human being? Why were people so selfish? All of these questions were going through my head with no answers to be found.

The love I'd experienced with David was profound but I had to accept that I'd gotten, somehow, a glimpse into the heavenly realms of love that didn't exist here on earth. Yet I knew that type of love is what I'd been seeking my whole life. I had experienced it as a child. It was God's love and it was pure and beautiful.

I realized I could be grateful to have experienced that kind of love with another, even if it was in another realm. But I wasn't sure if David could be the one for me. He had a long road of recovery ahead of him. I didn't think I could make the transition from a healing partner to a romantic partner. I'd recently learned he had two young daughters, and I didn't know what was going on there. Plus, my two boys and I had many challenges ahead, which took all of my energy. Along with my school demands, I wouldn't have time to help David in his healing journey any further. Real love was letting go. So why did I feel so sad?

Later that day, David called. He said he'd see me at the Thursday AA meeting and he had my linens ready to return then. He said he was feeling better and looked forward to seeing me. My spirit brightened at the thought of seeing him.

Chapter 28

Checking In

Friday, October 28, 2005

I saw David last night at the AA meeting. He had brought my linens back but realized he had left a sheet out. He asked if I might be willing to drop by after my class to pick it up. I offered to bring lunch too if he would like. He said, "Yeah, that'd be great. I'll pay for it though. My treat."

The next day I picked up some Thai food from a restaurant near my class and headed over to see him. He was doing much better now and even able to walk with a cane, having gotten beyond the need for a walker. He told me that someone from the program had given him a plane ticket to go visit his family on the West Coast. He would be gone for two weeks, leaving on Thursday, November 3 and coming back on Wednesday, November 16.

His eyes grew misty as he talked about how lovingly supported he had been throughout all of this by his many friends in AA, and also how much he appreciated the healing care I had provided. I was worried about him flying so soon while he was still very weak. His illness had been exacerbated by his previous flights when one of his ears didn't pop to relieve the air pressure from his last trip. The cascading events that led to him nearly dying seemed related and

I was very concerned that this could cause a relapse. Each time I wanted to let go, I found myself more drawn to making sure he would really be okay.

The medications he was taking were making him weak. Those included steroids and chemotherapy in the form of anti-cancer medications (Cytoxan), and Methotrexate, usually used for treating rheumatoid arthritis, to help keep the inflammatory response down because that was the treatment protocol for Wegener's Granulomatosis. David had lost his body hair and beard as a side effect. Although the blood clots had dissolved, the doctor felt he needed to be on a popular blood thinner just to be on the safe side. That, too, was having side effects. David had also been taking an antidepressant prior to his illness. He had lost about 35 pounds while he was in the coma and still had a diminished appetite, so I was worried he was underweight and undernourished, too. And now he was going to travel.

I shared my concerns with him and in response he asked if we could work together to help get his energy level in better shape before he left. I said I'd do what I could.

David lay down on the couch and I began working with him as I had in the hospital. The energy started flowing from him to me and then back again. We were both enfolded within it.

David could feel his hands heating up. "What's going on?"

"That's the healing energy coming through. It looks like you're a healer, too."

"But I don't know anything about that."

I explained to him that people who had a near-death experience like he did often came back with heightened awareness, healing gifts, or extra-sensory abilities.

"I've always felt there was something more like this, just it was out of my reach," he said. "Now it makes more sense to me."

"It seems to me then that you came back with a healing ability."

He said he understood about healing, having been exposed to it through Unity, but he had never experienced anything like this before our work together. Then he began opening up more.

"I work in the securities business."

"So do you own a gun?"

He laughed. "I meant in the financial services area."

I didn't quite know what he meant until he said stocks and bonds. That much I understood.

"I started working on the trading floor of the San Francisco Exchange as a runner when I was 19. Then I worked my way up to being a professional trader. I've worked in this biz my whole life."

"And what about now?"

"I came to Richmond in February to work as a contractor for a major securities firm here. It was supposed to be for a year, but they offered me a full-time job starting in September. But then I got sick."

"Did they hold your job for you or are you going to go back West and make a fresh start?"

"My boss has been great and the people I worked with have, too. They're holding my job for me. After I get back from this trip I'm going back to work."

Selfishly, I was excited to hear that he was coming back, or at least at that moment he thought he would. But I knew anything could happen when he got out to see his family. And he was still very ill.

When he'd mentioned his work team, I remembered how I'd seen cards in his hospital room and how Frank had said that David's colleagues had conducted fundraisers to help him out. They sounded like good people and he was lucky to have such a supportive work environment.

I could tell David was growing tired and needed to rest. As I got up to leave I told him I'd spend as much time as I could over the coming days to work with him before he left.

His AA sponsor, Dan, was speaking the next evening, Saturday night, and he asked if I would come and listen with him.

"Sure David, thanks. I'll see you there."

CHAPTER 29
MOVING ALONG

Saturday, October 29, 2005

The speaker was starting at eight. David came in with Sheila and several other people from AA. He said they'd had dinner before the meeting. He asked why I didn't come to the dinner.

"I didn't know about it or I would have."

"Oops, I meant to invite you but must have been too nervous to remember."

I laughed and we sat down together, with David seated to my right. I said something to him, but he didn't seem to hear. I gently nudged him: "It's great to see Dan, isn't it?" He agreed. Then I said something else and again he didn't respond.

"David?"

No response. He was staring ahead.

I nudged him. "Did you hear me?"

"No," he replied. "I think they said there's something wrong with the hearing in my left ear, because all I can hear is a ringing noise."

We later found out that David's nerves had been damaged and that he had completely lost hearing in his left ear. We didn't know if it would come back. The power of the healing interactions in the hospital, but especially during the shared near-death encounter, had not been replicated since. I wondered why his ear hadn't healed and if there could be any help for it.

David's energy level was still very low and walking even a few paces caused him to breathe heavily. After the meeting, we hugged goodbye. He asked if I would come by on Monday and I said I would.

CHAPTER 30
HEALING TOUCH TOGETHER

October 31 through November 2, 2005

I visited David over the next three days, continuing to work with his energy field and help him strengthen. We would talk afterward and he would share more of his life with me. He told me about how unhappy he'd been, his drinking, his sobriety for the past year, and that he didn't know what was going to happen next with anything.

He talked about his two daughters. About the money he'd made; the great cars, the Hawaiian vacations, the custom-built homes, and how he'd lost it all due to his drinking and eventual job losses. He had taken a new job and made a fresh start in the Pacific Northwest and within 10 months of the move, the firm shut down for a securities violation and he was out of work in a new city with no savings. He struggled to find another job. It was there he realized he needed to turn his life around, get and stay sober, and he began to attend AA meetings. Quickly, his life started to turn around and the contract offer for the job in Richmond came his way. It took months for it to actually get set up and then he came here in February.

On his last trip back to Richmond in June, after visiting his family out West, he had noticed when he got off the plane that his left ear didn't pop. Shortly after, the headaches started, and then also a sensitivity to light. He had to wear sunglasses in the office because the bright lights hurt his eyes. Then he developed Bell's Palsy, which is partial paralysis of the facial muscles. As he became progressively sicker, the doctors couldn't figure out what was going on.

Then the rest happened and here he was, trying to figure out what happened and what was going to happen next.

He talked about his life, his mom, his dad, his brother and his experiences as a young boy growing up in San Francisco. He talked about his mother, Mama Dee, and how she had gotten pregnant with him when she was 19, shortly after his parents had married. The family had moved to Israel when David was seven to live on a kibbutz. But the marriage was strained and after a year, the family returned. David's parents divorced; his mom remarried, but her own drinking worsened. Finally, his mom realized she was an alcoholic and that she might also be a lesbian. Soon after, she got sober, came out and had been living with her partner, Jane, for the past 25 years.

David said his life in the financial services biz led to a lifestyle of partying and hard drinking. Even with his mother's experience in AA, he didn't listen at the time. When things inevitably fell apart though, he finally went to an AA meeting. And that's where he finally felt he belonged.

"You've been given a second chance," I said. "You can turn this all around and I'll pray that's what happens for you."

On the day before he was going to leave, he seemed better but he was still very weak. As I was working with him, he put his hand on my hip. The energy that shot through us with that connection caused us both to shake uncontrollably. His hand was hot and the energy coming through him was increasing mine, too. Then the love I'd felt in that dimension came flooding through us both.

"I don't know what this means but there is such love here. And the healing coming from your hands is amazing," I said.

He looked at me. "I feel it, too."

"I don't think it's a boy, girl thing. I think we had this experience so we could help others and use these healing abilities to draw people closer to God."

"I don't know what it is, but I know it's real."

"Look, I know you are going tomorrow. I want what's best for you, no matter what that is. I don't know what this is, but it's out of our hands. I made a commitment to serve God in the best way I can and I'm doing my best to do that. I'll keep those prayers going for your highest and best." After a soothing moment of silence between us, I asked, "Will you drop me an email and let me know how you're doing?"

"I will do that."

We hugged goodbye. Once at home I tried to sort out the confusing emotions I was feeling. The love I'd felt with him during the shared near-death experience had now surrounded us both in our real lives, in our physical bodies. And it felt just as powerful as it had in that dimension. I was stunned to feel it so profoundly and was also terrified that I wouldn't feel it again. Was it tied to David? Or was he just showing me the way? Was it possible that this kind of love could exist in this earthly life? The experience was a conscious contact with the God of love that I'd always believed in and although I'd had glimpses and moments, I hadn't felt it with another person in this way before. Had the healing encounter just expanded my capacity to feel this higher love?

I didn't know the answers. But what did I know was that I had to trust God to work it out. When I told David it was out of our hands, I meant it. This whole experience was not of me and him. There was a force of love so great that it brought us together and now here we were. If this love could bring us together, bring David back from near death, and open his healing gifts and expand my heart, that might be all that we get in this life. I needed to be more grateful beginning with thankfulness for having time to think about things while he was gone over the next two weeks.

CHAPTER 31
TIME APART

November 3 through 16, 2005

The next days went by in a blur. I was busy with school, the boys were both doing better in school and in life, and I was preparing for the Thanksgiving holiday. I had more speakers to line up for the rest of the semester, including Esther, who was willing to speak on her experience as a Holocaust survivor and how she had turned to love and helping others as the keys to her healing. She was a philanthropist now and used her money to provide scholarships for students in the pharmacy school where her beloved husband had taught. Esther was going to speak on a Friday, two days after David was scheduled to return.

I'd gotten one email from David while he was visiting his mother is San Francisco. He said the breeze from the Pacific was healing for him and that he was enjoying his time there. He closed with, "I miss the warmth of your hands and the healing time we've shared."

I wrote back, "I'm glad to hear you're doing well." At the end of my note I wrote, "I'll continue my prayers for your very highest and best at all times."

But I didn't hear from him again and felt a twinge of disappointment. He was due back on November 16, but as that day came to a close I did not hear from him. Although I felt let down, I also felt that the prayers I'd made were answered and that I had to let go. Still, there was a part of me that remained connected even during this time apart. I realized I missed David and the honest conversations we had shared.

CHAPTER 32
KISS ME

Thursday, November 17, 2005

As I got out of my car and walked to the entrance for an AA meeting, I saw David standing there, leaning on his cane, waiting for me. He looked at me and said, "Kiss me."

That was the last thing I expected him to say. I gave him a little peck. "I'll bet you say that to all the girls."

We laughed and went in together. The meeting was good. Afterwards, I told him that Esther was going to speak the next day in my class and I invited him to come. I thought he might appreciate the Jewish history she would share, and I told him that he would be welcome to join us for lunch after class if he chose to come.

He said he would love to come and I told him where to meet me before the class. I hugged him goodbye and went home excited about the next day.

Chapter 33
Today's Lesson: Forgiveness

Friday, November 18, 2005

The next day before my class, David met me and we walked over together. David was leaving heavily on his cane, but his color was good and he looked like he felt so much better. I introduced him to Esther before the class began. After David sat down, Esther pulled me aside and told me about the concept of the Jewish soul mate called a "bashert."

"That's what you and David are. Before this life, you were created to be together. Finding each other is a gift. It is a union like no other."

Esther gave a great talk to the class, sharing her experience of the Holocaust as a young child, and how she survived during it and in its aftermath. She talked about flying planes when she served in the Israeli army. She also talked about not understanding money and that when she told her father that she wanted to understand finances better, he laughed at her. She became a school psychologist instead, earning her Ph.D. in counseling psychology. She later became a financial advisor for a major securities firm and made millions of dollars. She talked about the importance of giving back and helping others. "Forgiveness is central to living a rich life," she said.

When the class ended, Esther, David and I walked over to a Thai restaurant for lunch. During the conversation David talked about how his trip to San Francisco and breathing in the sea air had been healing for him. As if on cue, Esther reached for her purse and pulled out the keys to her condo on the oceanfront in Norfolk. I had helped her with some of the cleanup when she bought it, so now she wanted David and me to take the keys and go for the day and breathe in some of that fresh sea air. David said he would love to go. And I said that I would enjoy it too, but I was coming down with a nasty cold and wasn't sure if it would be good for me to go and expose him to my germs. "I'll check with you in the morning and see how I'm feeling," I told him. As I walked with him back to his car, he said, "I don't care about your germs, I just want you to go with me."

CHAPTER 34

LOVING CONNECTION

Saturday, November 19, 2005

The next morning, I got up and was coughing uncontrollably. I called David and told him I didn't think I could go. But he would have none of it. I found some cough drops and then drove over to pick him up and found him sitting on his front porch with his little bag beside him.

"I couldn't sleep last night because I was so excited," he said. His childlike honesty touched me. I'd been used to men being aloof, so for him to be waiting on the porch like an excited schoolboy was endearing.

During the drive to Norfolk, David wanted to hold my hand. Then he put his hand on my head and was rubbing my hair. As soon as we got to the condo David leaned in and kissed me. I wasn't sure what to do. He was still very shaky. And I was very sick. So, we decided to take a nap. I found my coughing was under control enough so that I might be able to rest.

I thought of being with David but knew it was way too soon. Besides, we were both ill. I turned to my side and felt David gently pull me toward him.

"Please, make love to me," he said.

"It's too soon."

"I don't know how much time I have left."

He leaned in to kiss me.

"Wait," I said. I put my hand on his heart. I put my face close to his.

"Breathe me," I said. We began to breathe together, my hand on his heart and his on mine. We looked into each other's eyes and the energy started to flow and swirl all around us. I was engulfed in the love we felt in that other dimension. He felt it, too.

We touched each other gently and when our bodies joined, we experienced the explosion of love so strongly that we shook with the force of it.

Immediately after, David started to cry. "What's wrong?" I asked, alarmed.

"Would you get my medicine? I'm a guy. I don't want you to see me cry."

"Of course, but please tell me what's wrong." I had said I thought it was too soon and now feared he was filled with regret.

"I didn't know it could be like that," he said. "I didn't know I could feel that kind of love."

I brushed away his tears. "I didn't either."

"I want to be with you for the next 20 years," David said.

"What happens after 20 years? You'll trade me in?"

We both laughed. Twenty years seemed far away and all we had was today. We held on to each other throughout the night.

We had to leave the next day because David was speaking at a meeting at eight that evening. On the ride back, he asked me to turn the heater on as high as it would go. He was shivering and said he was cold to the bone. Then he said he wasn't feeling well. I apologized, thinking that being together had made him worse or that my germs had gotten to him. He refused that apology, saying being with me made him feel better and that he would be okay.

I went with him to the meeting and as we were parting, we talked about Thanksgiving coming up on Thursday. I invited him to come to my house for dinner. I had told him about Ryan and James and that it might not be a very peaceful dinner. I was nervous about how it would go, whether the boys would like David, and whether David would be able to handle them.

"I'd love to. Thank you."

We hugged goodbye and I headed home. I was in love. It was possible to bring that love we'd found on the other side and experience it in our hearts and bodies. It did exist and I was overjoyed.

Chapter 35
Another Relapse

November 21 through 23, 2005

The next day David and I talked. He said he wasn't feeling well and was going to see his doctor on Tuesday. I offered to bring him lunch and he said that would be nice. When I came by, he opened the door and looked terrible. His skin looked gray, he was shaking all over and he was having trouble standing.

"I'm sorry, but I don't think I can eat and I need to rest," he said.

I was still sick myself, so I decided that I had better leave fast and not expose him to any more of my germs. I asked him to let me know how he was doing.

The next day I called David to check on him, but there was no answer. I felt alarm coursing through me. Something was wrong and I could feel it. I prayed.

That afternoon, he called me. He was back in the hospital, this time with double pneumonia. The medication had reduced his immune response so much that now he was deathly ill again. He wasn't allowed visitors because the doctors didn't want him exposed to anyone.

But the next day was Thanksgiving, so I asked, "Would you like me to bring you a Thanksgiving meal?"

"Yes, that would be nice. Thanks."

We talked a bit more. I could hear in his voice that he was tired. I was worried.

When I got to the store to get fixings for Thanksgiving dinner, I saw Lenny, who was a butcher in the meat department. Lenny and I had chatted over the years and I had told him about David. He had a strong Christian faith and would tell me that God worked everything out. I told him what had happened and how David and I had fallen in love and now he was deathly sick again. I said I was afraid and sad. It seemed so odd to find this kind of love and now it could be snatched away.

Lenny said, "God decides how long you will get to keep this. Even if it's only for a day, it's the kind of love most people never experience. If that's all God allows, be grateful you could experience it at all."

I realized Lenny was right. I wanted this love to last forever. But it wasn't up to me. Just as I'd told David, this was out of our hands and in God's. Whatever happened was up to God. I had to accept the love that I had been shown and not be greedy. If this was it, if this love that we had shared showed me that just for a time, love like that could exist, then it would have to be enough.

I went home and planned the meal for the next day.

Chapter 36
One more Chance

Thursday, November 24, 2005, Thanksgiving Day

I had an early dinner with the boys. I told them about David and how I had hoped they might meet him today, but that he was still very sick. James poked Ryan with a turkey leg and they both giggled. I was glad they were having fun and enjoying our time together. I had told them about David when I was visiting him. They knew I had worked with other people, so they weren't as curious about it as they might have been. They enjoyed the turkey and sides and were excited about going to Tim's for the rest of the day, where they were going to have a second feast at dinner time. I made a plate for David, dropped the boys off at Tim's and headed over to the hospital.

When I got there, Sheila was coming out the front door. She said that she had brought David a Thanksgiving plate but he couldn't eat anything. She was upset and worried about him.

The nurses gave me a protective mask to wear in order to go in to see David. He was back in the CCU and I saw Nurse Sherrie there.

"What's going on?"

"It's double pneumonia, but he's also having a reaction to some of the medicine. The doctor is cutting it way back to help his immune system stabilize."

"Is he going to be okay?"

"We're doing our best to help but he's very weak. Keep those prayers coming."

I went in to see David. He did not look well and I was worried, too. I hugged him and he hugged me. I could see he was weak and tired. He thanked me for the meal, but said he didn't have much appetite. He was breathing in short breaths and it seemed he was having trouble doing that. I asked Nurse Sherrie to come look.

She called the doctor and they ordered oxygen for him. I felt terribly guilty, certain that my germs had made him sick. I shared my concerns with Nurse Sherrie. "It's not your fault. His medications made him susceptible to germs and he's still not one hundred percent well. Personally, I don't think the recent plane rides were a good idea and probably had more to do with this." She suggested that I go home now so he could rest. My cold had cleared up by then and Nurse Sherrie's words soothed me.

Worried about David, I went home and prayed. Even though I agreed with what Lenny said about being grateful for the time David and I had shared, the truth was, I was angry. I felt like someone had held out the greatest gift I could imagine and then snatched it away. David and I had experienced a miracle and I didn't know if it would happen again.

Chapter 37

I Love You

Friday, November 25, 2005

The next morning at 6:30, the phone rang. I jumped out of bed to hear David's voice on the other line. His breathing was shallow and I could tell he was struggling.

"I don't know if I'm going to make it," he said. "Can I tell you I love you? I want you to know that now."

"I love you, too," I said.

"Will you come?"

"I'm on my way." I brushed my teeth and quickly dressed.

When I got to the hospital I found that David had been moved to another room. I was told to put the protective mask on again, and when I went in he looked very gray. "Would you come here and hold me?" he asked.

I helped him sit up and then I crawled onto the hospital bed beside him and held on to him for dear life. The love we'd felt embraced us both. I could feel the Reiki energy going from my body to his and back again. I continued to hold him, and then I noticed that his breathing became easier and longer.

I began to breathe with him and we breathed together. Soon he said he was feeling better and I moved off the bed so he could rest.

The next few days he recovered, bit by bit. The boys spent the weekend with Tim and I stayed with David as much as I could. We talked more about our lives, about what had happened, about all of our hopes and dreams. There was no time for pretending. Our conversations were raw and honest.

Then he told me about a woman he'd met before he got sick. He really liked her and had thought there might be something there. He told me he had called her to come visit and was waiting to see if she might call back. I asked him if that's who he wanted to be with and for him to be honest about it. I struggled to accept that what he and I had experienced was surreal and had happened quickly and that maybe that was really all we were going to have together. I told him to think about what he wanted and that maybe he needed to explore that.

I told him that I needed to go and think about some things too. After what I had believed was a shared experience that had profoundly bonded both of us, it seemed that David wanted someone else. While my mind was trying to find a foothold in understanding, the truth was I felt punched in the gut. I thought we were bonded in every way. To think he wanted to be with someone else made me doubt that we were meant to be together. I wanted to be all loving, but I was hurt that he didn't seem to feel the way I thought he had.

David called later to let me know he was doing much better. I told him I was glad to hear it. I was feeling down about things now and wanted to get off the phone quickly so I could think more. He said he'd check in with me tomorrow and he'd love to see me because there were some things he wanted to talk with me about. I said I'd come see him.

Chapter 38
Life on Life's Terms

Saturday and Sunday, November 26 and 27, 2005

David and I spent the days and evenings talking about life, choices and what was next. He said that he was still processing through everything and that what had happened with us was so surprising that he was doing his best now to deal with it.

He talked about how he was going about his life, getting sicker, feeling sadder, and how he had met this woman whom he thought he could at some point have a relationship with. And while he loved me, he had to close out their budding relationship because it was where he had left off when he got sick.

I understood. I still had lingering feelings for Greg and wondered if this was happening because David and I weren't meant to be together. I still loved David, though. I didn't have a choice. It just was.

David talked about how much recovery he had ahead. The double pneumonia was clearing up and his prognosis looked good. He talked about how he had lost everything. About how he didn't feel he had anything to offer me.

"You've got nowhere to go but up," I affirmed. "You can get your health back and get money again, but only you know what's in your heart. And I know that this kind of love is a gift. I'm grateful for what we had."

I wasn't sure now what the future held in store for me, or for him, but I had to let go and let love lead the way.

CHAPTER 39
BANANA SPLITS

Monday, November 28, 2005

I had a job interview scheduled at three that afternoon for a position with the State of Virginia. The job would entail working with the morgue and performing case analysis and reporting. I wasn't thrilled with it, but I needed steady income and health insurance. I had budgeted to finish my Ph.D. program in two and a half to three years, but now my dissertation was moving slowly and I wasn't feeling much passion about it. I felt I was being led in a different direction, but with all my course work completed, my comprehensive examinations out of the way, and my dissertation proposal accepted, I felt I needed to move forward with it.

David was still in the hospital, but improving steadily. We were hoping he'd be able to go home the next day.

I went to the interview and learned that my analysis would be focused on violent deaths and violence prevention strategies. The workspace would be a few floors above the morgue. After talking with the panel of five people, they asked me to do a 15-minute timed writing test—it would be to craft a public relations announcement about a particular health-related issue. Leading me to a small room, the interviewer handed me a paper with the facts of the case and I typed away on the computer they had provided.

When I was done, David called to check in about how it had gone. I told him I did my best and would see if it worked out. He asked me how I'd feel having my workspace being a few floors up from the morgue, given how sensitive I was.

"I wouldn't choose to be alone in the building at night, but I can handle it during the day. And if I have a visitor, I'll pray for them to go to the light of love and peace."

The conversation then shifted to how he was doing. David said that the doctors told him he was looking so much better today. They were testing his Wegener's marker (this was called a C-ANCA test) to see if it was still positive and if the disease was still active.

I told him I would see him later that night after having dinner with a friend of mine, and asked him if he wanted me to bring anything.

"I'd love a banana split."

"Sure. A Baskin-Robbins is next door to where I'm meeting my friend for dinner so it will be easy for me to run by on my way over." When I stopped off to get it, though, a thunderous downpour had started. I ran from the car and was soaked in the sprint to the counter. I ordered two banana splits to go and dashed back to the car. By the time I got to the hospital, driving slowly in the torrential rain, the ice cream and I had melted.

David and I ate the melted mess out of the little cups and talked. His doctor came in and said he had some good news to report. David's C-ANCA tests came back negative. David was in remission! The doctor said he would need to remain on some of the medications, but at a reduced amount. They would also continue to monitor his health after discharge, which was scheduled for the next day.

Chapter 40
Lessons from a Local Writer

Thursday, December 1, 2005

I had a guest speaker coming to my Marriage and Family class the next day. Richmond author Jewel Cherise (this is her real name) had published her book about life in urban communities, unprotected sex and the consequences of HIV and AIDS—in particular how AIDS was plaguing the African-American community. She talked to the students about some of the issues teens were facing today, including the risks of unplanned pregnancy, about building self-esteem and having a vision and purpose in life.

She read a few powerful passages from her recent book. The honesty of her writing encouraged the class to talk more about the issues and pressures they were dealing with. The discussion was so engaging that the students wanted to know if Jewel could come back. Since we were wrapping up the semester and preparing for exams, I didn't have any additional guest speakers scheduled. The following week was open and Jewel agreed to come back.

After class, Jewel and I went to lunch. We talked about her dreams and I shared with her what had been going on with David. She looked me in the eyes and said, "You are destined to be together. None of this would have happened if you weren't." The intensity in her eyes bored through me and I felt the truth of her words.

She continued, "He was headed down a wrong path and that's why he got sick. But God's grace pulled him through and if he's willing to open his eyes, you can be happy together."

Later, David called to tell me he was going home from the hospital.

Chapter 41
Life Speeds Up

November through December 2005

After David went home, the weeks went by in a blur. We saw each other every day and talked, shared, held each other, and continued to heal. The energy between us was surprising, especially when it seemed to come out of nowhere. When he would sleep, I would keep my hands on his back and they would stay hot. The healing energy seemed to pour out of me and I let it.

I was busy bringing the semester to a close. With Jewel as the guest speaker the week before, we had one more class discussion, which would be on the topic of human sexuality. Students were often shy about asking those kinds of questions, so I told them to write their questions down and put them in the basket that I was passing around. They wouldn't need to use their names, so they could ask whatever they really wanted to know.

As I drew their pieces of paper out of the basket, themes began to emerge. Questions centered around penis size. And women's orgasms and how to tell if you'd had one. I shared with the class the statistics that not many women are able to have orgasms from intercourse alone, so in that case, penis size didn't really matter. Our textbook had good references, but it was no substitute for an open discussion. We also talked about sexuality and its many expressions including pornography. The class had mixed views on this topic ranging from disgust to it's okay and it has its place.

One area that no one had seemed to have heard of was sacred sexuality. This included tantric sexuality, which was an expression of higher consciousness and loving union. It is deeply intimate and requires trust and love. We talked about this as being an important part of a relationship. We wrapped up with the love styles model put forward by psychologist John Alan Lee that we'd discussed at the beginning of the semester.

The following week was scheduled for exams and we would be done. David's birthday was coming up too, on December 16. We had plans to celebrate with our recovery friends at a nice dinner.

Chapter 42
Birthday Dinner

Friday, December 16, 2005

The birthday dinner was filled with fun, and David was laughing and having a great time. The friends who had been there through the whole journey with David came out to celebrate. As we went around the table to share birthday wishes, David took time to thank everyone for the love, prayers, support, and fellowship they had given him.

"I didn't know when I came to Richmond that I would nearly die," he said. "And I didn't know that I would have a second chance to live. And to find love in so many ways and from so many people. I love you all."

"We love you, David," everyone said at once.

When the dinner was over, we went back to my condo. David was tired but happy.

We talked about the journey so far and what was next. He said he was starting to clear his mind now that he'd had time to recover. He then told me what was in his heart.

"When I first opened my eyes at the hospital and saw you, I was instantly in love with you with every fiber of my being. I knew everything about you at a deep soul level. I didn't know how or why because we'd never met, but I did. I knew I was meant to be with you for the rest of our journey together. I knew all of this, but I didn't know how it would happen, because I was still sick and wasn't sure I was even going to live. I know I'm in remission now and I don't know how long it will last. But I know whatever time I have left, I'd like to spend it with you."

"Are you sure? What about the woman you told me about? This may be too soon and you need time to heal."

"I'm not interested in anything with that other person. It's not where I'm meant to go. I'm meant to be with you and I want to be with you forever if you'll have me," David said. "I know in my soul I came back for you."

Tears were streaming down my face now. David and I had found a connection, joined in a love that was greater than either of us. He had awakened a love in me that had long been dormant. He had brought back my ability to feel pure love. He had shared with me his near-death experience, his life, and shown me a world of love on the other side that had healed him and healed me.

After all the years of heartache with men and relationships, instability and pain, David was offering to bring me love in its highest and best way. I didn't need a provider. I needed a lover, friend, soulmate, and partner. And I needed someone who would be a positive influence on my boys. David wanted to be that man and I knew my boys would like him.

David and I snuggled in together, feeling the love flow between us. He stayed with me that night and never left. I knew the road ahead would be hard. But we could walk it together, every day, waking up to love.

EPILOGUE

I taught my Marriage and Family class again in the spring semester of 2006. I brought many of the same speakers back and added some new ones. The students in my class continued to amaze me with their openness, smarts, and willingness to think about love and life in different ways.

David started back to work soon after his birthday. Although he was still recovering slowly, he wanted to get back into the flow of things.

We married on June 30, 2006.

Our journey has been challenging on many levels, but we have continued to walk it together. Our children have grown up and we have grown older. My career path took an interesting turn into the financial services field. I studied women and the psychology around money and investing. I researched their attitudes, perceptions, and behaviors and ended up completing my PhD research in this field. As I continue in my healing work, I have found that revitalization is needed in every area of our lives: our finances, spirits, emotions, relationships, and health.

When David got better, I promised to the God of my understanding that I would dedicate my life to healing. I didn't understand why I had ended up moving away from hands-on healing and into the financial services field, but it certainly had helped us get through the many hard years and expenses.

Now David and I are sharing our story publicly and speaking about the healing power of love. During the past several years, I have worked with other critically ill people hovering on the brink of death. I am happy to say many of these individuals made stunning recoveries. I believe that what I have learned can help others heal, and I plan to devote the rest of my life to doing just that.

David and I continue to learn and grow. We have both maintained our sobriety and are dedicated to recovery and helping others in AA and Al-Anon. We're sharing our story now because the world needs love, compassion, recovery and healing more than ever.

We have one main message: that love is the greatest force in the universe.

If you're looking to find it, know that the love you seek is already within you. The love that has no words is all around you. You are made of love. You are love. Breathe it in. Breathe it out. Let love be your guiding light. We were born to love. We are here to learn how to love ourselves, one another, and our Creator.

Whenever you feel lonely, turn to love and know you're not alone. There are forces in this universe that love you more than you can even comprehend.

Whenever you turn to something for comfort, something that actually makes you sick, reach out for love instead. The hand of love will reach back and take yours.

May you find comfort and peace in waking up to love.

ABOUT SCARLETT
L. HEINBUCH, PH.D.

Dr. Scarlett L. Heinbuch holds a Ph.D. in public policy from Virginia Commonwealth University and a master's degree in public health from VCU's School of Medicine. She is a certified Reiki Master in the Usui System of Natural Healing. She has studied complementary, alternative, and integrative medicine for more than 25 years and is an energy practitioner. She is a pioneering researcher in the area of women and money, especially as it relates to women's attitudes and behaviors around retirement planning, which is the topic of her PhD dissertation. In addition to energy healing, she has worked in the financial services field for more than 15 years, bringing compassion and love to the workplace. She and David Schwartz live in Richmond, Virginia, where they are both active in the recovery community. For more information, please visit her website at: www.scarlettheinbuch.com